Praise for *Changing Shoes*:

"When Tina and I first started in soaps we were both the young temptresses. In her fabulous and entertaining book, *Changing Shoes*, she shows us that even though our roles as actress, wife, daughter, and mother may change as time goes on, with the right attitude—and shoes—we can stay sexy and relevant and take on new challenges, whether we're dancing with the stars or climbing Mount Kilimanjaro."

—Susan Lucci, Emmy Award–winning star of *All My Children*

"Tina Sloan LOVES shoes—what woman doesn't! But her feeling that the right pair makes you feel really special becomes a clever metaphor for stepping into life's ups and downs with a healthy attitude. *Changing Shoes* is a breezy, thoughtful perspective on how to enjoy life fully."

—Arie L. Kopelman, vice chairman of Chanel, Inc.

"For twenty years I watched the glamorous Tina Sloan play Nurse Lillian Raines on *Guiding Light*. Little did I know that as she retired in to middle age, she'd write a book with an irresistible title. (How could Tina know shoes are my weak point and greatest indulgence?) *Changing Shoes*, which discusses the challenges of getting older with dignity, style, and humor, is now my latest indulgent weakness. I love the casual philosophies herein. A terrific book for any woman who thinks she can't go on without Botox."

—Liz Smith

"Exhilarating! Tina's life is relatable to women of all ages as she struggles and overcomes life's challenges by simply refusing to give up and by wearing the right pair of shoes."

—Annette de la Renta

"Actress-author Tina Sloan advises women not to let life walk all over them. Her message is not to allow aging to defeat you or slow you down, to stop mourning your lost youth and to find a new, fabulous pair of shoes that fit your life."

—*Pittsburgh Post-Gazette*

"Soap star becomes a guiding light for women in [this] new book."

—*Newsday*

COURTESY OF THE AUTHOR

For twenty-six years, **Tina Sloan** played the role of Nurse Lillian Raines on *Guiding Light*, which aired its final episode in 2009 after a seventy-two-year run on radio and television. She has appeared on many other television shows, including *Third Watch* and *Law & Order: SVU*, and in a variety of feature films, including *The Brave One* and *Changing Lanes*. She is currently shooting two feature films and touring nationally in her acclaimed one-woman show, *Changing Shoes*. She lives in New York with her husband, Steve McPherson. They have one son, Renny.

Changing Shoes

Stayng in the Game
with Style, Humor, and Grace

Tina Sloan

GOTHAM BOOKS

GOTHAM BOOKS
Published by Penguin Group (USA) Inc.
375 Hudson Street, New York, New York 10014, U.S.A.

Penguin Group (Canada), 90 Eglinton Avenue East, Suite 700, Toronto, Ontario M4P 2Y3, Canada (a division of Pearson Penguin Canada Inc.) · Penguin Books Ltd, 80 Strand, London WC2R 0RL, England · Penguin Ireland, 25 St Stephen's Green, Dublin 2, Ireland (a division of Penguin Books Ltd) · Penguin Group (Australia), 250 Camberwell Road, Camberwell, Victoria 3124, Australia (a division of Pearson Australia Group Pty Ltd) · Penguin Books India Pvt Ltd, 11 Community Centre, Panchsheel Park, New Delhi–110 017, India · Penguin Group (NZ), 67 Apollo Drive, Rosedale, Auckland 0632, New Zealand (a division of Pearson New Zealand Ltd) · Penguin Books (South Africa) (Pty) Ltd, 24 Sturdee Avenue, Rosebank, Johannesburg 2196, South Africa

Penguin Books Ltd, Registered Offices: 80 Strand, London WC2R 0RL, England

Published by Gotham Books, a member of Penguin Group (USA) Inc.

Previously published as a Gotham Books hardcover edition

First trade paperback printing, August 2011

1 3 5 7 9 10 8 6 4 2

Gotham Books and the skyscraper logo are trademarks of Penguin Group (USA) Inc.

THE LIBRARY OF CONGRESS HAS CATALOGED THIS BOOK AS FOLLOWS:
Sloan, Tina.
Changing shoes : staying in the game with style, humor, and grace / Tina Sloan.
p.   cm.
ISBN 978-1-592-40568-8 (hbk.)   978-1-592-40664-7 (pbk)
1. Middle-aged women—Psychology. 2. Aging—Psychological aspects. 3. Self-esteem in women.
4. Sloan, Tina. I. Title.
HQ1059.4.S498   2010
305.244'20973—dc22   2010015281

Printed in the United States of America
Set in Centaur MT with Ribbon Display • Designed by Elke Sigal

While the author has made every effort to provide accurate telephone numbers and Internet addresses at the time of publication, neither the publisher nor the author assumes any responsibility for errors, or for changes that occur after publication. Further, the publisher does not have any control over and does not assume any responsibility for author or third-party Web sites or their content..

In the beginning
Jessica Noyes, Meg Pearson, James Benkard

•

In the middle
Joe Plummer, Wendy Sherman, Lauren Marino—
there would be no book without you all

•

In the end
Ann Campbell, the editor of all editors,
who made it all happen

•

And as always, to Steve and Renny,
for beginnings, middles, and ends

Contents

Changing Shoes

CHAPTER ONE

Staying in the Game

*I*t was at age forty-eight that I was struck by the proverbial clap of thunder, the kind that forces you to do a bald-faced reevaluation of your life. It was ten in the morning and I was walking down Forty-fourth Street in Manhattan with my soap opera daughter, Beth Chamberlin, to get a cup of coffee. We were in evening gowns because our last scene had been a gala party where we were murdering someone. (Most likely the someone we were murdering was asking for too much money in his contract.) "Oh, Beth, you were so great in that scene! The way you stabbed him thirty-two times, I loved it. Thank heavens you didn't get any blood on my gown!" I said, laughing. I was feeling fabulous and beautiful, wearing dripping diamond earrings, Christian Louboutin heels, and an Oscar de la Renta canary yellow gown.

I loved to be spotted outside in my costume, as though my character had suddenly broken through the fourth wall and come to life. Beth and I would waltz outside after our scenes in whatever garb we were wearing, be it bloody medical scrubs, pajamas, or elegant designer gowns, and run and get some fresh air. Even in a city like New York, where people have seen it all, our appearance on the street always elicited a lot of attention.

As a woman and an actress no less, I know when I'm being watched. I would feel the covert glances of strangers assessing me, and let's admit it, for any woman, this can be a thrill. But this time, standing there in the coffee shop waiting for my double tall mochaccino to be delivered, I could sense that something was wrong. Looking around the coffee shop, nothing seemed to be out of place . . . sugars, creamers, straws, napkins—everything was where it was supposed to be . . . what could be wrong?

Then I saw him. The man with the salt-and-pepper hair in the corner of the coffee shop, perfectly dressed in an Armani blue blazer, yellow Hermès tie, and gold cuff links, staring fixedly at Beth. I followed the trajectory of his eyes and there could be no doubt, he was staring at her, the way men used to stare at me. If he had been pointing a pistol at me it would not have been as terrifying. Glancing around, I understood what was making me feel uneasy. NO ONE was looking at me. NO ONE. They were ALL looking at Beth. The handsome man in the corner, the man making our coffee, who was so transfixed he scalded himself with the hot milk, the three girls in line behind us with their yoga mats, even the little red-haired boy and his two friends—obviously playing hooky—were watching her. The whole coffee shop was enthralled with Beth. Nobody even glanced at me.

I hated her.

After getting back to my dressing room, I looked in the mirror and was astounded. How—in ONE day—had I gotten old? And more important, how had I not noticed the wrinkles and soft arms? I was close to fifty, and yes, I had been coloring my hair for years, but somehow, I'd always thought that other than that, I was just fine.

For the first time in years, sitting there in front of my dressing room mirror, I thought about Aga Church.

Aga Church had been my muse many years ago. She was a Parisian friend of my parents, with whom I had spent a summer when I was in my twenties. At the time, my mother and I were locked in an epic battle over my future: I wanted to become an actress; she wanted me to find a husband, buy a house, get a golden retriever, and start bringing up children. Like so many well-bred women of her generation, my mother had put her own interests on hold when she married my father, and she was adamant that I forget this "silly nonsense" about acting and choose a more dignified path. "Darling, why would you ever want to be an actress?" she asked. "Acting is so ... *déclassé*. There are practical considerations that a girl your age has to think about. It's time for you to grow up, my dear." In order to escape my mother's clucks of disapproval and constant monitoring eye, I jumped at the chance to travel to Paris.

How—in ONE day—had I gotten old?

I think my parents had hoped that Aga would talk some sense into me. They couldn't have been more mistaken. To me Aga was the epitome of female independence. She looked like she had stepped out of a fashion magazine. Her hair was always perfectly coiffed, her clothes were impeccable, and she was so self-assured, so confident, so alive. For Aga, even spreading jam on a croissant was an act filled with style and flair. She opened my eyes to a world so different from that of my sheltered, suburban upbringing. It was the 1960s and she had invested in a fabulous Parisian nightclub called The Crazy Horse where the most beautiful women I had ever seen danced—and took off their clothes! We were there every night and we were treated like royalty; Aga moved among the crowd as if she was Marie Antoinette herself. She seemed to float through the room, between acts, smoking her ubiquitous French cigarettes, sipping her Dom Perignon, and chatting with her friends. I watched her and studied her every move.

Since we never got up before one o'clock, it was late afternoon the day Aga took me to Chanel. She wanted to buy me some new shoes. I will never forget watching her walking through the store, pointing to different pairs of shoes, each lovelier than the last, and saying: "These shoes are for simply having fun—nothing serious, a brief rendezvous. And these are for when you want a man to notice you, but not fall in love with you. And these shoes, Tina, these shoes are for seduction!" Aga's relationship to shoes was a revelation. In her mind, each experience in a woman's life corresponded with a different pair of shoes, and she had seemingly walked in them all.

After a moment Aga turned to me, motioned to the wall of shoes before us, and in her thick French accent said, "Now, Tina, you choose." I didn't know what to do. There were so many choices. I walked along the wall taking one shoe and then another in my hand. They were so beautiful and the heels were so high, the soles were smooth and they were so light. I had always wanted to own a pair of expensive high heels. I had sneaked out of the house a few times in a pair of my mother's old spectators that never really fit me. But here was Aga, offering me, for the very first time in my life, my own pair of designer high heels. It didn't take long for me to spot the ones I wanted. The moment I saw them I knew they were The Ones. They were classic and black and they seemed to me like a work of art.

When I first kicked off my college-girl Capezios and slipped on those black Chanel heels, I felt as if the world around me was transformed and everything suddenly became more exciting. I wore those shoes as I walked the streets of the Sixteenth Arrondissement, where Aga lived, from Rue Saint-Honoré to the Left Bank, learning about art and architecture and French culture and, of course, under Aga's tutelage, men. I felt free and giddy with possibility, certain that those shoes would take me somewhere fabulous. They were my magic shoes. Over the course of that summer, Aga taught me about life and how to really live. And she ultimately gave me the courage to go against my mother's wishes and to become an actress. At a time when I wasn't sure if I had choices, Aga taught me that a woman must always have the choice when it comes to her shoes. She would say, "Tina, the hardest part is knowing which shoes to wear—once you know that, all the rest is just *marché*. But always make sure that the shoes you wear are your own. That way your feet will know where to take you." She showed me that the world was my oyster—accompanied by Champagne, naturally.

> *Always make sure that the shoes you wear are your own.*

When I returned to New York, my feet knew where to take me. Every time I put on those Chanel heels, I felt that same sense of glamour and confidence I'd felt in Paris. I was wearing them the day I got my first role in a television commercial and the day I got my first part in a soap opera. And when they wore out I had others like them, glorious heels, thin ones in dark colors for everyday, and gold and silver ones for parties. I even wore stylish Chanel white heels with my nurse's uniform during my early days on

Guiding Light. I remembered the words that Aga told me, and I chose shoes that took me to all sorts of fascinating places and introduced me to all sorts of wonderful people.

There's an expression in French called the *coup de vieux*, the "blow of age," when one suddenly looks old. Many years later when I returned to Paris to visit this stylish and gorgeous woman, she had disappeared. Aga came into the bar where my husband and I sat. In she walked, this tiny, frail woman. Gone were the stunning clothes and shoes; no one said hello to her or recognized her or fussed over the way they always had when I'd been with her years ago. Aga had aged, but even worse, she seemed to have given up. It devastated me. I felt angry at her. I felt betrayed. I couldn't understand it, of course. Later I would learn more about what Aga was going through and have more sympathy. But at that time I just couldn't grasp what had happened.

I was young then. Now on this day in the coffee shop with Beth, nearing fifty, I realized that I had become that woman—the one who's invisible, even in the to-die-for evening gown.

Around this time I also began dealing with other things that were making me feel my true age. Everywhere I turned, there seemed to be signs that my life was changing, and not for the better. My parents' health was in decline. My son had recently joined the Marines and would be going to Iraq. My skin was duller. My body was softer. My role on *Guiding Light* had been fading away right under my nose. Gone were the skimpy dresses and love interests—it was the plots that were skimpy now. All my lines were about other characters, not me. And my shoes, which now that I looked more closely, were usually the same pair of scuffed and broken-in black flats, complete with cushions from

Dr. Scholl's. I no longer cared which shoes I wore—forget glamour and confidence—I just wanted to be comfortable. Wearing heels had begun to make my feet hurt ... then my legs ... then my back. I'd even started wearing sneakers on *Guiding Light* because they were much more comfy and went with the scrubs that nurses were beginning to wear. They were practical shoes, and I'd succumbed to practicality.

For a while I felt paralyzed, overwhelmed by the new reality that was rapidly unfolding before my eyes. I felt as if I were facing a huge desert of quicksand, and I needed to learn how to navigate it, or jump on a camel and cross it, but I didn't know where to find a map or a camel—even in New York City where we have everything. This sense of paralysis lasted for almost a year, but I was at a turning point in my life and I couldn't just keep denying it. The landscape around me was changing, and I had to move forward—but how?

I looked around for role models who could offer me guidance for this next phase and was largely dismayed by what I saw. In most parts of our society, the idea of "aging gracefully" seemed to be equated with "gracefully" heading out to pasture. I began to notice how older people were usually overlooked, even at their own parties, be it a wedding anniversary or birthday. My own mother had gone on living a quiet life in the suburbs, watching her friends drift away and leaving most of the daily decisions and details to my father while her health and mind deteriorated. On the flip side, I noticed the women walking around my neighborhood who had been Botoxed and nip-tucked to within an inch of their life, desperately fighting a war they couldn't win. Neither of these roads appealed to me. I wanted to stay in the game and continue to feel productive and vital and beautiful.

Even my friends seemed conflicted about how to approach

aging. My friend Jean called me up one day, having just taken her life's collection of Guccis and Manolo Blahniks and donated them to the local thrift store. "I'm down to my lowest kitten heel," she informed me. It was a practical decision, fueled by aching feet and the fact that closet space in New York City is highly prized. But my other friend Anne, who is in her sixties, always, always, always wears high heels. She can't help herself. And if you ask her why, she'll say, "I just feel good in them." One woman's common-sense adjustment is another woman's unthinkable sacrifice. Do we accept our age because in not doing so we deny a very real part of ourselves? Or do we fight with everything we have to hang on to the same life we've always known?

Fortunately, I'd had a great-aunt who had been a very famous decorator in her time—she had done the sets for the Folies Bergère—and had lived a rich and wonderful life well into her eighties. As a child, I would go to dinner at her house once a week and watched her hold court among her successful, elegant friends, who included Elizabeth Arden and Rose Cumming, one of the founding doyennes of modern interior design. And even after my aunt had stopped working, her home retained an air of energy and vibrancy. She entertained constantly, was always up on current events and front and center in any intellectual discussion, and above all, she was always beautifully dressed. She had one exquisite outfit that suited her perfectly and that she'd had made in every fabric and color imaginable, and she paired it with the most lovely mules right up until the day she died. I decided that her genes were the ones I had in me—and that I wouldn't let her down. I also remembered a note Aga had written me thirty years earlier when I was equally confused about where my life was headed. I realized that the advice was just as applicable now:

Dear Tina,
If you cannot hear the voice inside of you, it
just means it's time to get a new pair of shoes.

This book is about how I learned to navigate the desert of aging with my dignity, sanity, and sense of style intact (and, against all Hollywood rules, WITHOUT plastic surgery). It is about how we can find the courage to transform ourselves and learn to twinkle again, even after the lights have dimmed. From our looks to our love lives, from our identities to our careers, I have learned that it IS possible to stay in the game as we age. We can continue growing and learning and making a difference to those around us. The years ahead are ours to own and cherish. We cannot let anything, least of all our age, stand in our way!

> *The years ahead are ours to own and cherish.*

Throughout this book, I share the stories of my own challenges and missteps—some hilarious, some extremely painful—as I found my oases in the desert of aging, along with the stories of many of my friends who are redefining what it means to be a woman in this phase of life, and demonstrating every single day that it doesn't just have to be about losing our power or fighting wrinkles (although a great face cream definitely helps). I've made my own rules and found a way to embrace these years as both an enormous test of what I'm made of, and a gift that brings new freedoms, pleasures, and possibilities—and yes, great shoes. There were times in recent years when I opened up my closet and didn't even yearn for the high heels, but now I fight back and wear high heels again. Yes, they are a LOT lower than they were in my younger days, but I love the feeling they give me—that I can laugh in the face of aging, that I am living my life once more.

These days, if you look in my closet, you'll find heels, flats, Grecian sandals, snow boots, all of Lillian's shoes from *Guiding Light*, and even a pair of tap shoes that never came out of the box. I like open shoes, because I don't like being constricted, so almost all my shoes have an opening in the toe or at the back. What could be a better way to make sure that we remain open to all areas of life?

And yes, on occasion, I still do wear the high, high heels because at the end of the day they make me feel glamorous. I love seeing my reflection in store windows as I parade past. I think that, as women, it's part of our DNA to strut our stuff. Even though they might give us headaches or bad knees, or make our feet hurt, we are drawn to heels because they somehow elevate us above our everyday reality. They give us height, stature, a little lift in the world. Ultimately, we wear high heels because they bring us closer to the stars.

It is my hope that this book—written in the wee hours of the morning since, as every woman my age knows, one doesn't sleep—will be your guide to changing shoes, to the transitions that inevitably come with getting older. And I hope that through my experiences and those of my friends, you will find laughter, inspiration, and a lesson or two about how to change your shoes—or maybe change them back—with grace. This book is also a reminder to make sure that whatever shoes you wear, they are always, as Aga said, YOUR OWN. Maybe you honestly don't like heels. Maybe you never did. That's okay. This is not about my style—it's about yours. It's about making sure that who you are does not disappear in this next phase. We can be fifty or sixty or even much older and still retain the spark and zest of our younger days; we can seek out new friendships, relationships, and adventures, and our closets can inspire what we do today rather than remind us of who or what we once were. Like Nora Ephron, I feel bad about my neck, but what's the alternative? To die, as they say, with the music still in us.

Sometime shortly after my moment of revelation in the coffee shop with Beth, I did a film, *The Brave One*, with Jodie Foster. We were seated next to each other in the makeup chairs, and the makeup artist casually said that she was surprised and impressed that I'd never had any plastic surgery. "And I don't have any plans to get any either," I told her. The room went totally quiet for a minute, and then Jodie looked at me and said, "Tina, thank God there are women like you out in front for the rest of us."

I KNOW aging is part of life as it spins down. And I know sixty is NOT the new forty. It is sixty with all those lessons. We are aging and we can't resist it, but we can resist losing ourselves.

How? you ask. The answer is simple: You just have to change your shoes!

CHAPTER TWO

High Heels, Not Botox

It was a bright, sunny morning and I had just bounded out of my college dorm room dressed in a pretty pink A-line skirt and a new pair of Pappagallo shoes. I was on my way to meet two girl-friends for lunch. We had already spent the entire morning together up on the roof of the dorms sunning ourselves, coated in baby oil and holding our tin-foil trays out in front of us, three blond sputniks, making sure we had the perfect tans to go with the new outfits we had just bought the day before. Sure, exams were just around the corner, but the gorgeous weather was calling us sirenlike outside, and we, devout sun worshippers all, were powerless to resist. We were planning to meet at a little outdoor café that we loved, and I was running a few minutes late.

Hurrying along, giddy and ravenous—being out in the sun always made me so hungry—I was crossing the street when suddenly I heard a loud screech and a crunching sound. Looking up, I saw two cars stopped in the intersection. One, a lemon yellow

Studebaker, had plowed into the rear bumper of a black Lincoln, which had apparently slowed down while making a turn. The two male drivers were stepping out of their cars to survey the damage when a matronly woman standing beside me, who had obviously seen everything, said to me with a slightly resentful air, "They were watching you, honey!"

Watching ME? How marvelous! I waltzed gleefully into the restaurant and announced to my friends that I had caused my very first accident. One of my friends became quite cross—she didn't think I should be laughing over something so serious. But I thought it was absolutely hilarious and a great compliment. Here I was, twenty years old, without a care in the world, and I had literally stopped traffic—just by being me. And it didn't hurt that the two men, although older, were very attractive.

In those days, being young and beautiful was something that I took for granted. My looks were simply part and parcel of everything that, for me, made life one ongoing, wonderful adventure. They enabled me to have FUN. I had boyfriends galore and could always talk myself out of any trouble I got into (my whole life, I never, ever got a speeding ticket).

After those carefree college days, I moved to New York City despite my mother's protests. With Aga as my muse and my black Chanel heels for inspiration, I got a job as a typist at a law firm and started trying to figure out how to become an actress—and how to type; I don't know which one was harder. At the time, I knew almost no one in the theater except for one friend from college who was a playwright. I had no idea where to begin.

So I started calling the offices of every agent in town and asking for an appointment. The secretary would say, "Send us a photo of yourself first." So I did, and then I would call back and ask, "Did you get my photo and resume?" And the secretary would inevitably say, "Oh, send it again." So I would, and I would keep calling, and finally I would get in to meet the agent. I made at least forty phone calls a day—so many that I actually had to make a chart to keep track of them all. But no one wanted to represent me: I didn't have enough experience.

After months of typing and trying to get auditions, my college friend, the playwright, agreed to meet me at Schrafft's for a hot fudge sundae one afternoon. I hardly recognized him behind his full flowing beard and long hair; it had been over a year since we had seen each other and he had really changed. "John? Is that you?" I asked, still scrubbed and shiny in my new Peck & Peck lime green dress and matching clutch. "Tina!" he said sweetly. "You look beautiful." Settling into the booth I instantly poured my heart out to John while gobbling my hot fudge sundae. "Why can't I even get an audition?" John looked at me straight in the eye and said something I will never forget: "Tina, I'm going to give you three lines in my new play, but what you have to understand is that acting isn't just about dressing up, it's about being true." I had no idea what he was talking about, but who cared—I was in a play!

The play was so far off-Broadway it felt like Weehawken, but it didn't matter. It was a play, and I was in it! I was cast as a nine-months-pregnant woman, with three lines—"My water broke. I need to go to the hospital. Someone please help!"—and I loved every minute of it. I invited everyone I knew to see the play—agents, casting directors, my parents, friends, ex-boyfriends, current boyfriends, men I hoped to have as boyfriends. A few days after the show ended, I got a call from Gayle, a casting director at a small agency. She'd seen me in the play and wanted me to audition for a commercial. I had no clue what to expect from the audition, but I was ready to give it a try.

I snuck out of the law firm on my lunch hour and walked to the casting office. I was wearing my black Chanel heels (too bad the office was in a five-floor walk-up). When I arrived, there were dozens of other girls there ready to read for the same part, each one prettier than the last. They all eyed me up and down as I walked through the door huffing and puffing from the climb. I felt as though I had just walked into the middle of a birthday party that no one had invited me to. "I'm here to see Gayle," I announced to the room nervously as though they had all been waiting for me to get started. There was silence. A door opened and out walked a short, frenetic woman with a pair of eyeglasses in one hand and a pile of papers in the other. She looked at me and said, "Sign in." Then she shouted, "Next," and one of the girls followed her into the room from which she had just emerged. I signed in and found a place to sit.

One by one the girls went in and came out. The room slowly emptied. I was the last one to go. I followed Gayle into the cramped little room where she handed me a copy of the script—which was one line—and directed me to stand in front of the camera. "All right, Tina," she said, "whenever you're ready."

I took a deep breath, smiled, and in my best voice with perfect diction, I read, "The big tea taste of Tetley Iced Tea. It grows on you."

Gayle looked at me. "That's good, honey, but this ain't Chekhov. Lighten it up a little bit, eh? Give me a smile, a little up with the lips, you know?" *Chekhov?* What was she talking about? I tried it again, this time with a smile. "The big tea taste of Tetley Iced Tea. It grows on you." "That's great, hon, we'll be in touch," Gayle said as I walked out of the room.

And they were. A few days later, I got the part!

After that first big break, I landed several other commercials:

Dove, Colgate, Maybelline. Soon I had an agent and was working enough that I could afford to give up my typist's job. More and more commercials continued to roll in:

Stove Top Stuffing: *Guess what's for dinner, kids?*

Tipparillo: *Should a lady offer a gentleman a Tipparillo?*

Windex: *Let the sun shine in!*

It was simple. I smiled, opened a box, a bottle, a can, or a tube, and I was done.

I felt like I'd found where I belonged. I would go on auditions during the day and then travel downtown to take acting classes at night. I still didn't have much money, but I loved the work and the certainty that I was on the right path. I found a darling little apartment in the Des Artistes, a famous building on the West Side that was only for artists and, back then, incredibly cheap. I had wonderful fun mingling with my artist neighbors, many of whom would go on to become very famous writers, directors, poets, and painters.

Of course not everything was perfect. My mother continued to be less than encouraging. "Darling, it's just so embarrassing to have you traipsing around the city trying to do what? Become a movie star? Don't be ridiculous. You aren't going to succeed and it isn't dignified. Those commercials make you look so silly. You should be concentrating on finding a husband, not running around on ski slopes in some television commercial asking, 'Who wants gum? Who wants gum?' It's time to grow up."

I was also finding that no matter how pretty I was, there were those for whom I would never be pretty enough. It goes without saying that looks are hugely important in the acting world, and for the first time, I was forced to really assess how I measured up. Suddenly being beautiful was, according to some, the single most important factor in whether or not I would succeed.

One afternoon I was called in to a very fancy modeling agency. I was being considered for a job as a spokesmodel for a huge ad campaign that paid more money than I ever imagined possible. Armed with only my confidence and my black Chanel heels, I arrived and was ushered into a room with twenty gorgeous women. None of us acknowledged one another or even made eye contact, but boy, were we checking each other out.

Finally the owner of the agency came in to see us. She asked us all to stand before her and then she strode purposefully down the line, looking us over, one by one.

"You, my dear, are much too heavy, lose twenty pounds.

"You don't have good bones, you'll never make it in this business.

"You look plastic, you don't have any character in that face.

"Your eyebrows need a better arch, and you have to change your hair color. I need blondes.

"You need to have your teeth capped, blonder, blonder!"

At last it was my turn. The agent put one perfectly manicured hand on my face and said, "You're pretty enough, but you need a nose job."

A nose job?

It had never occurred to me. I always liked my nose! What was wrong with my nose?

I raced home to my apartment and spent hours examining my nose in the mirror. She was right; my nose was huge. How had I never noticed it before? It was like a balloon! How had I gone all these years walking the streets and going on auditions without noticing how enormous my nose was? *Nose job. Nose job.* If the agency owner was right, I had to do something about this. I had to get a nose job and transform my nose into the desired aquiline shape.

I met with a number of plastic surgeons, all of whom were

more than willing to redo my nose for a huge fee. And a few weeks later, I found myself lying on a gurney in one of their offices, staring at the ceiling lights above me. The nurse was bustling around me, preparing for the procedure, asking if I had any questions and if I had someone to pick me up. Finally she handed me a hospital gown and said, "Okay, dear, I need you to undress and put this on. The gown opens in the back. And take off your shoes, you won't be needing those."

I looked down at my black Chanel heels, the same ones I'd bought in Paris, and the same ones I'd worn to every single audition and job I'd had since I'd arrived in New York. I started to remove them and then stopped. Maybe this is what Aga was talking about. *"Tina, always make sure the shoes you wear are your own."*

I stood up and said, "I can't do this. I'm leaving. If I don't wear these shoes my feet won't know where to go."

She looked at me like I'd totally lost my mind. But it didn't matter—I was out of there. I grabbed my belongings and walked out of the office, and with every step I felt better and better. I felt like me.

I didn't get the ad campaign, but I kept working. The fear that my nose was too big stayed with me, and at every audition it still crossed my mind, but I learned my lines, hit my mark, and kept getting cast. In the months that followed I learned I could spend the day in front of my mirror worrying about my nose or I could put on a great pair of shoes, forget my nose, and step boldly out into the world.

Over the years, I've tried all sorts of silly things in the name of looking good: tanning beds, sprinkles on my face, purple lipstick, purple nail polish (it was the eighties and I was turning forty so you figure it out). Some of it just looked silly and some was downright dangerous. But experimenting with different

looks—and identities—when you are younger is all part of growing up. By the time you are fifty or sixty you should know who
you are and what works for you. The irony is that just when you
think you've figured it all out, your body starts to change and you
have to figure it out all over again. The fact is, while looking good
has its place, it's feeling comfortable in your own skin—no matter
how wrinkled—that allows you the confidence to go out into the
world with that certain *je ne sais quoi*. A pretty face with no character, no personality, no intelligence, or no interesting things to say
is just bland, bland, bland. In the acting world we are paid to look
attractive, but the most interesting characters have more than just
a pretty face—they have depth and humanity. And we all know
humanity is nothing if not imperfect.

My friend Melissa, who is my age, conducted an experiment. For
a month, she kept track of how many hours it took her to maintain her looks—that is, to keep herself looking more or less the
same. Manicures, pedicures, hair coloring, hair cutting, waxing,
exercise, eyebrow tweezing, teeth whitening, skin moisturizing,
putting on makeup and taking it off, shopping for clothes, shopping for makeup, and let's not forget all the doctors and dentists
and gynecologists and mammograms and vitamins we now have
to work into our lives. All in all she spent one hundred and eighty-
two hours a month just trying to stay even—that's a lot of effort
just to hold the battle line at neutral.

I don't even do half of what Melissa does—I'll shave my legs
at home and do my own nails unless it's for a special occasion—
but like most women my age, I definitely do my fair share of
maintenance and upkeep. In fact, the older I get, the harder it is
to avoid devoting a ridiculous amount of time to these two all-

important words (maintenance and upkeep), which make us sound like a vacuum cleaner or an airplane engine. But as Mae West said, "It's better to be looked over than to be overlooked," so I keep at it, keep fighting the good fight, knowing all along that no matter how hard I fight, I am going to lose the battle eventually.

I will never forget the moment I realized just what a losing game it is. I was sitting in the makeup chair next to Heather Graham while shooting a movie called *The Guru*. There we were, chatting away, and I was looking at her in the mirror in front of us. She was so charming and I was completely captivated. In the middle of our conversation, I happened to glance at myself. Seeing my face next to hers—it took my breath away. I couldn't speak; I just stared straight ahead, stunned with the realization of how much I had changed. There she was, one of the great beauties of our time, with flawless young skin, bubbling over with enthusiasm and youth, and next to her I felt devastated and old.

The reality of being an older actress is that you see your face constantly juxtaposed against twenty- and thirty-something faces, as I did every day with my lovely soap opera daughter and granddaughter on *Guiding Light*. But I tried not to let myself dwell too much on how I once looked, telling myself, "Okay, Scarlett, get over it. You had your time in the sun."

Still, the reality checks are everywhere and sooner or later, if you want to remain "beautiful," you have to adjust to the changes that come with age whether you like it or not. There is nothing quite as embarrassing as a woman of a certain age squeezing, squishing, and stuffing herself into clothes she is clearly too old to be wearing. No one wants to be the one to tell her, but often it takes someone else to snap us out of it. For me, this turning point, sparked by my darling husband and son, came one Christmas about ten years ago during what is now affectionately known as THE SCENE.

We were all down in Florida for the holidays: Steve, me, Renny, Renny's girlfriend, my stepdaughter and her husband, and my two stepgrandchildren. The weather was perfect and after escaping New York's dreary winter we were all eager to shed our coats and woolly layers and hit the pool. The first day we were there, I slipped on my bright red Eres bathing suit as I usually did, grabbed my book and towel, and prepared to head outside. But when I walked out into the living room, Steve and Renny stopped talking.

"What?" I asked. They were both completely silent. They looked at each other, then back at me.

"WHAT??" I asked again. "What is it, what's wrong?"

"Nothing," they said, but the look on their faces said it all.

"Mom," Renny said, "I don't think you want to wear that suit anymore."

"Why?? What are you talking about?"

"It's just . . . oh, nothing, never mind."

I went back into the bedroom and looked at myself in the mirror with a fresh eye. I had crepey arms and crepey legs and thick hips and a huge tummy. Of course I shouldn't have been wearing that suit. I felt crushed. But this was my favorite bathing suit and it had been for years. This suit had never failed me before. I had felt glamorous and invincible in it, and had had plenty of adventures, sailing and swimming and water-skiing. But now, due to the extra pounds I had added over the past couple of years, it was stretched and out of shape—like me.

I kept the suit on that day, adding a blouse on top and pretending I hadn't gone to look at myself. But that was the defining moment that changed the way I looked at clothes. I was dressed so inappropriately for my age and my body. It was almost as though I had been walking around in a ballerina tutu and fairy wings like my four-year-old granddaughter. If Renny's oh-so-pretty girlfriend had walked in the door in the middle of that conversation I would have been horrified. My body had gone away and someone else's had replaced it—someone else who looked amazingly like my mother. It was time to face up to my new "older" body and make some adjustments.

"It's like seeing an old coconut," I was telling my friend Duane later. "You know, it's all brown and shriveled up and scrunched in. This isn't the coconut you want to present to the gods—they want the beautiful, firm, ripe coconut!" "That's right," Duane said. "Let's face it—neither of us is the virgin they're going to be throwing off the cliff anymore. But that's okay," she laughed. "We'll be the ones throwing her in."

When I got back to New York, I opened up my closet full of short, strapless dresses that clearly I would never wear again and started pulling them out, one by one. I sat on the floor in a heap of dresses and just sobbed, lamenting my lost youth and body. I had so many great memories in those clothes—"That's the dress I wore to the Emmy Awards one year, that's the dress I was wearing that time I met that really handsome man on a boat when I was twenty-four, that's the dress that Aga bought me at Chanel"—and the stories all just came flooding back. After a long cry, I finally wrapped them up, put them in a box, and called UPS to deliver them to a beautiful, firm, ripe coconut: my niece, Meg. Watching the UPS man haul my dresses away I felt certain I would spend the rest of my life in pants with elastic waistbands, and T-shirts. "What difference does it make what I wear?" I asked myself as the man drove away with my youth and all my memories.

Of course, it matters what you wear. As luck would have it, the minute you give up on yourself and step outside looking like an old coconut—unkempt with dirty hair and no makeup, wearing yoga pants and a T-shirt—you are guaranteed to bump into The One Who Got Away. And that's exactly what happened to me the very next day. I was on my way to the gym when I ran into HIM. He of course looked impeccable in his khaki pants, Ferragamo belt, and lavender tailored Lacoste shirt tucked in. I was completely disheveled, and when I spotted him I instantly turned and walked into the nearest deli for fear he would see me. Standing there breathless by the cantaloupes, I felt as if I were in a bad detective novel. What had my life become? Of course he headed straight toward me. He had seen me! I started to walk quickly toward the back of the store when I heard his voice. "Tina? I thought it was you, but I wasn't sure. How are you?"

I was trapped. I tried to play it off. "Never better," I replied unconvincingly, and after a few moments of stilted conversation I escaped. But there was no getting around it, he had caught me looking my worst. Racing home, I had no doubt he had immediately called his wife and said, "Boy, am I glad I married you." My run-in had taught me a valuable lesson.

My friend Denise had a similar wake-up call when she went to her usual market one day without her makeup on. When they asked for her account, she was surprised and said, "It's me, Mrs. Crane." And the man behind the counter said, "Oh, you're Mrs. Crane's mother!" That was the end for her. She never went out of the house without makeup again.

As Meryl Streep's character says in *The Devil Wears Prada* when she cuts down her young assistant for scoffing at fashion, "You

> *Whenever I see someone who is older but still looks divine, it reminds me that maintenance is power. It keeps us visible; it keeps us being SEEN.*

can decide to opt out of fashion and beauty, but don't think that everyone around you will recognize this as an earnest act of defiance." Instead, they might just see a drab and lifeless-looking person and treat you accordingly. The fact is that we are wired as humans to prioritize or dismiss people based on appearances. And if we want to be noticed in a positive light, if we want to be taken for a person of consequence, especially as we age, we need to make the effort.

Whenever I see someone who is older but still looks divine, it reminds me that maintenance is power. It keeps us visible; it keeps us being SEEN. When I go to see Laura Norman, the guru of reflexology, for a session, I come out feeling AND looking younger, relaxed, and happier! I met a ninety-six-year-old woman on a plane recently who was looking fabulous with her pale pink lipstick, Chanel flats, and tan knit pantsuit. You could just tell that for her, it wasn't over. At ninety-six, she must have had a lot of aches and pains and loneliness, but she was working the *New York Times* crossword as though she hadn't a care in the world. She went to pull down her own suitcase when we landed, even though I'd offered to get it. "How do you do it?" I finally asked her. And she answered, "You just do."

So how do we deal with it? How do we avoid looking like that shriveled old coconut without becoming ridiculous or spending a fortune on the latest highly touted secrets of youth?

In the acting world, plastic surgery is usually the go-to remedy for aging stars. Our lives are in our looks, so who can blame us? Many actresses today start lifting and tweaking as early as their twenties and thirties and continue right on as they get older. But just because it's de rigueur in the business, doesn't mean everyone wants to admit it. Years ago, when I was on the soap opera *Search for Tomorrow,* I shared a dressing room with a beautiful young actress. One day she came back from vacation with bosoms she'd never had before. So I said, "Look what you got!" And she gave me no response. I found it absolutely astonishing. If you share a dressing room with someone for months and all of a sudden they have bosoms when they'd never had any before, how can you not comment on it? But she looked at me like she had no idea what I was talking about.

When my soap opera daughter, Beth Chamberlin, was first starting out, she had a manager who, when he signed her, declared, "You'll have to get those fixed," motioning toward her breasts. "What do you mean, fixed?" she asked with surprise. "Don't worry," he replied without missing a beat, "I'll pay for the implants and you can pay me back out of the money you earn." Needless to say, she didn't sign the contract and he never became her manager. But with so many voices critiquing you from every angle, it can be tough to work in the business and remain true to who you are.

In Manhattan, too, plastic surgery is often the done thing after a certain age. I've been at lunches where everyone at the table was talking about their plastic surgeons, and I had nothing to say because I'd never done it. I couldn't be a part of the conversation. And I guess this is a part of why women do it: They want to fit in. While I would never judge anyone for having plastic surgery—if it makes you feel better and you really hate how you look, and you have the money, then why not?—I think doing it just because other women are doing it, or because society makes us feel that we can't compete if we don't, is a mistake. I'm comfortable with having a face that shows where I've been and what I've done. Besides, I've seen too many cautionary tales.

Years ago on *Guiding Light*, there was an actress who had had so many face-lifts that she would come in wearing a baseball cap because her hairline had moved so far back. She had to wear wigs as a result. It seemed crazy to me even then, but her fear of losing her looks was obviously so great that she had gone to extremes to maintain them. You see a lot of this in Hollywood. You see the before and after pictures of certain celebrities and you just shake your head and wonder why. WHY did they do that? The gorgeous eyes or expressive face that made them so spectacular in their younger days have disappeared. They might as well be wearing a mask now.

Every now and then, I see someone who has had a great face-lift and looks wonderful, and I contemplate taking the plunge. But then for some reason I just don't do it. I'm even afraid of Botox, as I like my lines. I'm an actress, so I want to be able to smile and frown with all those muscles that give a face expression. Once a year, I will put silicone in the really deep lines around my mouth and nose, but that's it. I played a part in a movie called *Changing Lanes* with Ben Affleck where I played Amanda Peet's mother and Sydney Pollack's wife, and I know I got the part because I looked more or less my age. To me, that's a pretty good reason to avoid drastic measures.

That's not to say, however, that I'm above trying all sorts of noninvasive tricks to keep myself looking younger, and my skin looking a little brighter, a little tauter. The positive side of being in a profession that places such a great emphasis on looks is being regularly transformed at the hands of experts. For decades, I was lucky to have an entire team of hairstylists and makeup artists at my disposal. This, of course, was the hair and makeup team on *Guiding Light*. These people know all the tricks: They know exactly how to contour your face to define your jaw line, or hide the circles under your eyes, or make your skin appear perfectly sunkissed. If I had Joe or Helen or Paulie working on my face, and Ralphie or Linda fixing my hair every day, and following me around for touch-ups like they did when I was on the show, I'd look fabulous and youthful and radiant all the time.

On the set of a movie or a show like *Guiding Light*, the makeup chair is often the place to be. It's a social setup, with everyone seated in their chairs in front of the mirrors, and it's where gossip is exchanged, where you finally have a chance to find out who's doing what to whom in the next dressing room. And you'd hear some knockdown drag-out fights while you sat there, actresses sounding off on one another who, a little later, were happily working together.

I loved just plopping down in the chair and saying, "Make me beautiful, Joe," and he would come back with, "I ain't a magician," and go to work. The fact is Joe WAS a magician and taught me all sorts of tricks to make me look better, but even his magic had limits when it came to the effects of aging. Still, like every other woman in the world, I was certain that if I just found the right product, I could turn back the clock.

My friend CC knew lots of ways to make herself look magically better, and like most women, I'm a sucker for supposedly breakthrough miracle products. CC has the most perfect skin, and so, when she recently suggested that I try a new French face tightener, I jumped at the chance. She was always "to-ing and fro-ing" to France for work, so she was up on the latest things over there. And for me, the things "over there" spelled sophistication . . . they reminded me of Aga. The women of Paris weren't obsessed with losing their youth, they weren't always running to get plastic surgery. Sure, they would put on face tighteners, but they would keep their own faces. They loved being authentic. They were happy aging and sexy aging, and that was what I wanted—so if they used face tighteners, I wanted to use one, too.

CC offered me her top-secret source, so I trotted over to a hair salon on Madison Avenue—very chic—and asked for George. He greeted me with rapture and took me through the door in the back (I'd always wondered what goes on behind the closed door in every salon). It turns out that behind the door was a freezer: a place to keep hair color, lunch, and apparently, Popsicles. He handed me one. I said, "No, no, I want the face tightener." And he explained that for three hundred dollars cash, I had it. I should melt it a bit and slosh it all over my face, and then return it to the freezer. Hmmmm.

Well, I took it home, all two-and-a-half inches of it on a stick in a tiny seal pack (ten dollars extra) and stored it in my freezer, just as I'd been told. After checking with CC—and again admiring her skin—I figured I ought to give it a try. I lovingly took it out, set it on the kitchen counter, and let it start to get soft. The phone rang. Babble-babble-babble. I went to get dressed and as I was deftly applying eyeliner, I noticed my wrinkles and—yeek! I'd forgotten the Popsicle. I raced to the kitchen and there on the counter was . . . a little puddle of three hundred dollars. Pitifully I tried to slush it on my face, but too late, much too late. A Frenchwoman never would have done that, I thought mournfully.

There are times when our increased efforts to look nice and presentable can backfire in unexpected ways. I had a friend who was always beautifully dressed and accessorized; she wore earrings and jewelry and full makeup wherever she went, even to the doctor's office. One day she was getting ready to go to the gynecologist and she sprayed herself with some freshener "down there" to be sure she was all clean and presentable.

Well, during her exam, with her legs in the stirrups the doctor commented, "My, aren't we dressy today." She was flabbergasted, thinking to herself, "Dressy? What is he talking about, dressy? I have been seeing this doctor my whole life, what is he thinking? How dare he? I'm never going back to him again." Then she got home and realized that she had sprayed PURPLE GLITTER on herself rather than her freshening spray. Her grandchildren had been playing dress-up in her bathroom and had left the glitter spray behind. Oh, the perils of not wearing your reading glasses around the house. I guess *dressy* was a good word for her doctor to use after all.

The backfire for me happened with my hair. Hair is such a challenge for women as they get older. For many of us, myself included, our hair is our defining feature. Blonde is who I am, who I always have been. And often, just as in the story of Samson and Delilah, when we change or lose our hair, we feel as though we lose our power.

When I was a sophomore in high school, I had a best friend named Gloria, and both of us had long, blond hair. Everyone said we looked alike, which to me seemed an enormous compliment since Gloria was without question the coolest, most popular girl in school. Everything she did, I wanted to do, too, and we were always getting into trouble with the nuns at school, sneaking out of class to go to the movies or the beach. One time my mother even caught us hiding behind the forsythia bushes outside my house as the school bus drove by. She pretended to be furious, but I could tell she was trying not to laugh.

When Gloria arrived at school one day flaunting a dramatic new haircut, you can imagine the stir she caused. Astonishingly, she had shorn her gorgeous locks and replaced them with a VERY short haircut. This haircut even had a name—The DA (for Duck's Ass)—and just like a duck's bottom, her hair was combed straight back with a ruffle in the rear. But since Gloria was cool, this haircut was automatically the epitome of cool as well. She immediately suggested to me that I get the same cut—that way we'd be twins, just as we always had.

The name itself should have warned me off, but then again at age sixteen, nothing can warn you off. I agreed to Gloria's suggestion and went to her hairdresser and got the same cut. Unfortunately, since my hair was stick straight, it did not have any desire to stay pushed back or curl up at the bottom like an adorable little tail. It was no duck's ass—rather I looked like the Ugly Duckling. And I sure didn't look like Gloria. The haircut that was so dynamite on her was an absolute travesty on me.

Many years later, when I was thinking about my hair and whether or not I needed a change, this story flashed through my mind. I had given up my signature long, blond locks once—did I have the nerve to do it again? The conventional wisdom about hair on older women seems to be that we should cut it short. Even if we keep coloring it, shorter is better. From time to time, people would say to me, "Oh, you're too old to have long hair." One time I even arrived at a lunch with my hair pulled back and all my friends jumped up, saying, "Oh, thank goodness, you cut your hair!" But to me, long hair stands for femininity. To cut it off would be a sort of surrender, almost like announcing I wasn't going to try to be pretty anymore. I still like it, and I think it works. I can hide behind it, change it to suit my mood, and most important, it makes me feel like ME.

But I did think about changing the color when I first started going white—pure white—rather than just salt-and-pepper gray. I actually think snow white hair can be lovely on older women and I thought this look might be rather nice on me, and it would mean I could stop my bimonthly visits to the hairdresser to get the color touched up. All that coloring takes time and is expensive, so I decided I was just going to let the white grow in and see what happened. No one said a word until one day on *Guiding Light* when I was filming a courtroom scene. Peter Simon, who played Dr. Ed Bauer and was one of my favorite actors on the show, was standing behind me, and all of a sudden he said, "Okay, I can't stand it another minute. Tina, I'm sorry, but you look terrible with white hair."

I turned to him, stunned, but knowing he was right. "I'm sorry," he said again. "But I just think you should go back to blond. It's your thing." And

We need to be truthful about aging, but also true to ourselves.

it was true. My skin tone and coloring were all washed out; I looked like a white sheet or a white piece of paper or a white igloo or a polar bear. I was not a pretty woman with white hair. So I went blond again and have never looked back. Many women do look wonderful with white hair, but it wasn't for me. We need to be truthful about aging, but also true to ourselves.

Even when we know that we need to update our appearance, it can be hard to let go of the "old" you, especially if you've had a kind of signature look for years. We're often so used to seeing our hair styled one way and our makeup done in another that any change at all can be unnerving—even when everyone hastens to tell us it's for the better. Whenever I see those makeover stories on television or in women's magazines, I always wonder just how long it takes for the person to revert back to their old ways. We are all creatures of habit, and I don't think it matters whether it's your adoring husband and son or Anna Wintour herself who tells you that you just can't get away with that lipstick anymore—we often tune them out because we want to . . . or because, when we change too drastically, we just don't feel like US.

My friend Duane, who is in her sixties like me, orchestrated her own makeover several years ago after being shocked by what she called an "unfortunate" photograph. Suddenly, she found that her makeup looked too harsh, her hair too full—maybe even verging on the dreaded helmet head. "It's as though everything that used to work for me *doesn't* anymore," she told me. "But I wasn't worried. I decided to call in reinforcements."

For years, Duane had written for women's magazines, so she had an army of contacts in the hair, makeup, and fitness industries. She started with her beloved hairdresser of twenty-five years and asked her to give her an updated look, and followed that with makeup lessons from an artist who specialized in the cosmetology of aging. She was trimmed and styled and shaded and blended and freshened to the hilt, and she emerged with a new hairstyle— a sleeker, shorter cut with bangs—and a makeover feature in *Town & Country* to boot.

So how long did it last? "The bangs ended up driving me crazy," she said. "I was always pushing them back, and I never really got the hang of wielding all these brushes and blow-dryers in new, unfamiliar ways. I'm a hot curlers girl, I always have been, that's just me. But I did keep the new cheek color they gave me. It was called Orgasm, by Nars—I couldn't pass that up!"

Of course, the accessories we have to work with as we get older are a bit different than they used to be—and not always as sexy as a blush called Orgasm. These days, I always have a sweater with me in case I get cold—which is certainly NOT very sexy—but I need it with me even in warm weather, because air-conditioning drives me nuts. I get cold far more easily than I used to. Whenever my friends and I go to the movies, we all laugh because it might be a hundred degrees out but we bring along our sweaters just the same. And then there are the glasses. I wear them for reading and buy the cheap ones so I can have multiple pairs and keep them in every room so I don't lose them (another cliché that is all too true). But I'd rather spend another five dollars and have fun with a few different colors and styles of glasses than wander around all the time looking for them and feeling like an old fogey as a result.

And then there's the purse or handbag. For some inexplicable reason, women's purses seem to get bigger and bigger and heavier and heavier the older they get. I don't know what's in there, but my friend Duane's handbag probably weighs fifteen pounds. Personally, I think that we should all take a lesson from Coco Chanel who never, ever carried a handbag. She liked everything simple and came up with the idea of putting pockets in women's suit jackets so they could carry their money and other belongings right on them, just like a man. When I leave the house, I usually have my cell phone, my keys, a credit card, and a twenty-dollar bill. What else do I need? Sometimes I'll add a lipstick and a package of Kleenex, but even that's not necessary most days. It's much better for my back and saves me from getting that dreaded stoop that so many older women get. And good posture goes a long way toward making us look younger than our years.

Whether our makeover attempts work or not, the important

thing is to keep trying, keep looking at ourselves and asking what makes us feel good about our appearance. Just because some things about ourselves have changed it doesn't mean everything has to change. At the same time, if there are things we like about ourselves we should keep them—like my blond hair—no matter what anyone says. The important thing is to be true to yourself, to find the things that make you feel like you. It's like what my friend the playwright John had said to me all those years ago at Schrafft's: it isn't just about dressing up, it's about being true.

Tina's Tips for Looking Fabulous at Any Age

Find a Hairdresser Who Likes You. You want to go to someone who genuinely wants you to be beautiful. A good hairdresser will keep you up-to-date, but knows you well enough not to give you a Duck's Ass or some other cut that doesn't suit your personality.

Avoid Snow White Syndrome. Women who keep coloring their hair dark tend to look ridiculous after a certain age. Your skin tone changes and lightens as you get older, and suddenly your former hair color becomes too harsh for your complexion. Recognize that if you have always been a brunette, you likely need to go lighter now, or at least get some highlights to frame your face (like Diane Keaton's in *Something's Gotta Give*).

ALWAYS Wear Makeup. Remember the story about bumping into my old boyfriend and trying to hide in the cantaloupes. Lauren Hutton makes wonderful beauty products for aging women; they are available online and come with an instructional DVD that provides some great antiaging techniques and tricks. I also like Chantecaille and Bobbi Brown. I once met Bobbi Brown and she told me, "I make my products for your kind of woman."

... But Don't Overdo It. Nothing is less attractive than an older woman with bright pink cheeks. Plus, heavy makeup makes you look years older (and I think this is true as early as your thirties). At our age, less is more, so realize that you probably need to simplify your routine and start using more natural tones. If you're not sure how to do this, get a makeup professional to help you.

Avoid Powder on Your Face. Powder makes you look dry and settles in the creases in your skin, making wrinkles more prominent and you look older. Foundation or base is great since we need to even our skin tone out (like I do). And today there are so many good products available for older skin. Many of them multitask, providing antiaging ingredients along with an even skin tone and dewier skin.

Learn the Art of Contouring. With contouring, you're putting a darker color on the places where you want to create more definition, such as your jaw line. A makeup professional, or Lauren Hutton's instructional DVDs, can teach you how to do this.

Use White Around Your Eyes. The skin around the eyes thins as you get older, leaving you vulnerable to shadows and dark circles. Using white concealer on the inside corners and under your eyes will brighten your entire face and make your eyes look younger. Just make sure to blend it—mixing it with moisturizer if necessary—so you don't look like a startled jackrabbit.

Use an Eyelash Curler. Everyone should have an eyelash curler as there is no better way to open up your eyes and brighten your entire face, especially since the skin of the eyelid tends to thicken and droop over time. You can buy one for a few dollars at the drugstore. It will work best if you heat it before using it—simply run it under hot water or heat it with your blow-dryer. The words *thicken* and *droop* really upset me, but opening your eyes is kind of like a mini-face-lift!

Lighten Your Eyebrows. Much like your overall hair color, lighter brows are better as we age. You can lighten them with bleach and toner. To find the right shade of toner for your skin type, seek the advice of a professional, probably someone at your salon.

Get Your Teeth Whitened. When our teeth get yellowed, they age us tremendously, and coffee, tea, and red wine are all the culprits. You can get your teeth whitened by your dentist or use the at-home strips sold in drugstores, which do work, although not as well (but you can't beat the price).

Accessorize. A pretty colored scarf or earrings or a necklace can be a terrific way to liven up any outfit and announce to the world that you care about how you look. Accessories also work to camouflage our flaws: People will say, "Oh, what a pretty scarf!" and not, "Oh, she's put on a few pounds."

Find a Few "Uniforms" that Work for You. If you tend to just give in and throw on whatever shapeless, comfortable clothing is sitting on the chair, you are putting yourself at a disadvantage. You can avoid this and be chic anywhere, anytime by finding a few "looks" or combinations that work for you and wearing them often. For me, one uniform is beige or black slacks with a white shirt open, a blue blazer, a gorgeous chunky necklace, and big earrings—and pretty shoes, of course. You work it out and just keep wearing it, even when you are tempted to reach for the sweatpants and slippers. I find that when I'm dressed nicely, even if I'm just sitting at home, chances are I will find something exciting to do to make that outfit worthwhile.

· CHAPTER THREE ·

Forever Frisky

"*O*h my . . . oh my!"

I found myself murmuring these words in front of a roomful of onlookers, oblivious to their huge smiles. It had been at least ten years since I'd been kissed—really *kissed*—on the show, and the writers had finally decided to give my character, Nurse Lillian Raines, mother and grandmother on *Guiding Light,* a romantic story line. Somehow I thought I'd be immune to the power of a great kiss, even a scripted one, but when it finally happened in front of the cameras with my co-star Justin Deas, I was so unnerved that my lines flew straight out of my head. Flabbergasted, I froze on the spot, fumbling like a fool for something intelligible to say and all that came out was, "Oh my . . . oh my!" The producers were in hysterics over my candor. They loved it so much they decided to air the scene just as it was. My line was supposed to be some blasé retort, but the truth of the moment jarred me so unexpectedly that it came out differently than I had ever imagined. I wasn't the least blasé. I was totally overcome. I had been kissed, kissed by a new man. KISSED!

In reality, of course, I've been married for more than thirty-five years. And though my husband is the love of my life, I often think one of the hardest parts of getting older is missing the excitement—the butterflies, the giddy rush—that comes with romance and seduction when we're young. It all used to be so EASY. We could just fall into bed and stay there for days, take the phone off the hook, and order in pizza. Now pizza is the treat of our weekend. But, nothing makes a woman feel youthful and alive like the attentions of a man . . . or great sex.

When Lillian began dating Buzz Cooper, the change in her character was immediately apparent. Suddenly, she was glowing. She was thrilled to be KISSED and fawned over, brought flowers and given one man's undivided attention. No longer was she just fulfilling her role as nurse and taking care of everybody in the hospital and watching over her grandchildren. For once, she was not attending to someone else, but being attended to. She was being looked at and courted by a man her age. She was being SEEN. And that's really what it's all about, isn't it?

When I was in my twenties, I was "in love with love." Even during my college years, I had been somewhat famous—or infamous—for dating lots of different men. We'd all be in study hall, and someone would come in and announce, "Phone call!" and everybody would look up from their math or philosophy assignments, hoping, oh hoping that the person they were mad about was calling for them. And then they'd hear, "Tina Sloan, phone call!" I'd get up, take the call, come back, sit down, and then we'd hear again from the hallway—"Phone call!" everyone looks up, and then . . . "Tina Sloan, phone call!" Part of the problem, and the reason for so many of the phone calls, was that I could never say no when somebody asked me out, because I didn't want to hurt their feelings. I went out with one boy who was the heir to a huge electronics fortune—he was pale and awkward and not very attractive. But I felt so bad for him that I couldn't say no! Of course, this was the pre-sexual-revolution sixties, and you could go out on as many dates as you wanted because you never slept with anyone—you would make out, and that's all you did. (Although I most definitely did *not* make out with Mr. Electronics.)

There were times, though, when my romantic juggling got me into trouble. Once I had just started going out with a boy named Billy whom I really liked, and he asked me to come up to his college for the weekend. But I already had plans to go to Williams to see another boy that I was dating. Not wanting to hurt Billy's feelings, I told him that I was actually going to go home to spend time with my mother. I went off merrily to Williams for their Winter Weekend, convinced that I hadn't done any harm.

About three weeks later, I got a call from Billy. He said, "Tina, go get a copy of *Sports Illustrated*." He hung up before I even had a chance to ask why on earth I would want to read about sports, but I figured there must be a reason, so I set out to find a copy.

I went to the newsstand and was aghast when I saw the cover. There I was, making a snow castle with a bunch of other kids above a caption that read, "Williams' Winter Carnival." And of course the date of the weekend was right there in bold print—the same weekend I had supposedly been spending with my mother. Needless to say, things didn't continue with Billy after that, but I mean—*Sports Illustrated*—and the cover? I was thrilled! What are the chances? (Maybe if it had been the swimsuit issue, I'd still be dating Billy to this day.)

After I arrived in New York, and during the early days of my career, men continued to rule my life. I was obsessed with what they wanted and how to be interesting to them—and a lot of the time, they WERE interested, which made everything incredibly exciting. I dated a tennis pro and took up tennis. I dated a ski bum and started teaching skiing on the weekends in Vermont (well, let's be honest—I got the toddlers and walked them around on their tiny skis as they cried). I lived with a banker and I learned how to spend money (and ahhh, I learned it oh so well). I even lived with a bad-boy aspiring playwright who rode a motorcycle and brought adrenaline into my life.

One of my favorite dating experiences was with a man named Cliff, a fellow actor and poet. He had long wavy hair and black eyes and was heart-stoppingly gorgeous. He and I were in the same acting class, and we decided to use our dates as an opportunity to practice our craft. We'd pick a location, say Grand Central Station or the Montauk lighthouse on Long Island, and meet there and pretend we didn't know each other. And he'd say, "Oh, how do you do?" and I'd say, "How do you do?" And we'd make up stories about who we were. I'd be a student getting my master's in horticulture, and he'd be the governor of New York, or whoever else he wanted to be that day. And we'd go on for hours, all ad-libbed, and see who would lose the bluff first. It was so much fun because we could do all sorts of hilarious things—one time we were having dinner in a restaurant and I made a great scene and stormed out on him and he ran after me, and everyone around us just gaped. Part of the excitement was the challenge of it, which we both loved, but it was also the fact that every date was new. We had our first kiss together again and again—always as different characters, and always as thrilling.

On the other hand, one of the problems with my profession was the undesirable attention. In the acting world, there will always be casting directors or producers eager to "take advantage" of the young girl looking for her big break. I found this out first-hand when I got a call to go read to be a spokeswoman on a major television network. They had come up with the idea of having a young, attractive woman come on at the end of a show and tell people to stay tuned for the next show coming along. Back then, this was a brand-new concept. And to me it felt like the big-time. Every day I could go on TV and tell people to stay tuned for the next show and everyone would know who I was. The network was looking for energy and personality, and I was confident that I had oodles of both. Oh, that youthful confidence.

I went in and auditioned and it got down to four of us and I remember thinking how amazing it was that one of us was going to get this job. It paid soooo much money, and I just kept think-ing, "Well, why can't it be me?" After all, it didn't take too much talent, if any, to say "Stay tuned for..." and producers really wanted someone that viewers would like. I just knew I was perfect for it. Finally, it got down to two of us, and we were told that the final audition would be held the next morning.

As I was gathering up my belongings, the director came out of the audition room and started chatting with me. He was very cool-looking; wearing jeans, a green shirt with the collar turned up, and a leather jacket. Combined with the all-powerful air that directors usually have, he was devastatingly handsome to me. Of course I wanted to impress him with how likeable I was, so I was doing my damnedest to charm him. Maybe I was being a tad too charming as he soon suggested that we go out for a drink and din-ner. I knew that things had suddenly taken a turn when he put his hand a little too low on my waist and looked deeply into my eyes, and... uh oh! I didn't want to offend him, as he had real stature in the business, BUT I knew he was married. I had no idea how to handle a situation like this. I really, REALLY wanted the part, but I wasn't about to get involved with a married man. So I made up some excuse and said how lovely it was of him to ask me and how sorry I was that I couldn't go, and headed home flustered and prayed it would be all right.

The next morning, I arrived for the final audition all dressed and pressed and ready to give it my all. As I walked down the long hallway, the director emerged with the other girl and I just looked at them and there was no question—she had gone to dinner with him and now she had the job. It was all over both of them. The gazes they gave each other and the flinch of embarrassment she had when she saw me gave them away. He just looked smug. And he was wearing the SAME jeans and leather jacket and green shirt with the collar still turned up. He went through all the formalities of an audition, ushering me into the booth to do the final reading and giving me directions in a detached voice, and guess what? I didn't get the part. I was crushed, and it made me furious, too. My mother and father tried to console me but I was devastated by this glimpse of reality.

I was heartbroken, but I decided to reward myself for my "virtue" by going out and getting a new pair of shoes—gorgeous, strappy silver heels with a pale pink and lavender crisscross across the toe—that I found in a little boutique in Greenwich Village. I dubbed them my "Cinderella shoes" because every time I slipped them on, I felt like my fairy godmother had just waved her magic wand. The style, the shape, the curve of the heel, all made me feel beautiful and sexy. No matter what party I was headed to that evening, I knew that in those shoes, I would have a great time— and keep my virtue intact. My girlfriends and I would even joke about "The Shoes," as every time I wore them I seemed to meet a different man. They were constantly asking to borrow them.

> *No matter what party I was headed to that evening, I knew that in those shoes, I would have a great time.*

The energy I got from my Cinderella shoes carried over to my career as well. One day I was called in to audition for a soap opera. After losing the network job and being so disappointed, I decided that I needed to change my shoes and wear something other than my Chanel heels to the audition—so I wore my Cinderella shoes instead. And it worked! I got the part, a real character with a real name, not just "pretty girl" or "woman number two." I was Kate Thornton on the soap opera *Somerset*. She was the bad girl who had come on the show to steal the leading man away from his wholesome girlfriend. Kate was the publisher of the town's newspaper and Julian, the leading man, was the editor. The first thing she did when she arrived on the show was fire him.

The actor playing Julian was by far the handsomest man I had ever laid eyes on, and the first love scene I ever had on camera was with him. There we were, making out, madly, passionately, and my heart was pounding. He was so divine, so handsome, so sexy, and he even did the *New York Times* crossword puzzle—in ink. It was the first time I had ever kissed anyone on camera, and I could feel that this wasn't just acting—we were REALLY kissing! After the take, Julian leaned in close and whispered in my ear, "Tina, you're the first woman who's ever made me hard."

The first *woman*? Agh! I was heartbroken. Well, for a few days anyway.

Every day on *Somerset*, I got to throw on fabulous clothes and cause trouble in paradise. Kate would wear fur coats with nothing but lingerie underneath and skimpy dresses dripping with jewels. She had power and she knew it, and she did whatever she wanted to do. She even got pregnant with Julian's baby and didn't tell him and had an abortion, which was an extremely provocative story line at the time. It was the first time abortion had ever been discussed on daytime television. Ted Danson, later of *Cheers*, played the character who took me to the clinic. Of course, this still being the seventies, Kate had to be punished for what she'd done. She went crazy and ended up in a straitjacket in the loony bin, and from there her character was written off.

But it wasn't just the characters' lives that were rife with romantic tangles—there was plenty of intrigue behind the scenes as well. There's something about the closeness of soap operas— working long hours with your costars day after day and playing out these very emotionally intense scenes—that invites off-camera liaisons. After *Somerset*, when I was on *Another World*, I shared a dressing room with a girl who was having an affair with one of the other actors, who was married, and I could never get into the room to change. I'd knock on the door and get no response and finally I just started dressing elsewhere. But it was very tense because this man was one of the leading characters on the show, and I was playing opposite him on set. I was worried that he might not want to continue acting with me because he knew that *I* knew about the affair, and he could have easily had me written off. It felt very dangerous at the time.

For the most part, after Julian, I had learned my lesson about getting romantically involved with costars. Only once did I succumb to a workplace romance, and it was with this adorable boy on *Another World* who was much younger than me—by about ten years. I'd never dated anybody younger, but he hounded me all the time and was so cute that I finally gave in ... and went on a date with him. It wasn't worth it. It had no resonance at all. I felt like his therapist or career counselor. But it did make me realize that, perhaps for the first time, I was beginning to grow bored of all these breezy romances that were nothing more than fun and games. I wanted something deeper. I wanted to find love.

One evening, when I was in my early thirties, I went to a dinner party at the home of one of the producers on *Another World*. At that time on the show, I was playing Dr. Olivia Delaney—a "brilliant cardiologist" who had won the Nobel Prize (you'll note that doctors on soaps are always described as "brilliant" and often win Nobel Prizes). In real life, I was enjoying the fruits of my success in daytime television and dating a tango dancer from Buenos Aires, who was just as lighthearted and fun as all the men who had come before, but who was also smolderingly good-looking with an accent that kept me hanging on to his every word. He accompanied me to the producer's apartment that night and I couldn't wait to show him off.

I was wearing my Cinderella shoes, and at dinner, I found myself sitting next to a man named Steve. I was immediately struck by his presence: the timbre of his voice, the way he carried himself, his intelligence, his calm, his dimples, and his smile. Something inside me clicked, and the first thing I said to him was, "You're the man I'd like to marry!"

I was shocked by my own bluntness. The tango dancer stared at me, baffled, and said only, "*Que?*" Steve's date—well, you should have seen her face! But I couldn't help it. I knew that I wanted to know this man, and in my Cinderella shoes, I was brave enough to act. We talked through the entire meal, about everything from politics to astrology, and were still talking after the dessert and coffee had been cleared away. The next morning, February 1st—my birthday—a dozen red roses arrived with a note that said: *To Aquarius, Love Leo.* And every year since then I have received a dozen red roses on my birthday with the same note, from Steve, the Leo I married.

Our love affair was a whirlwind from the start. He took me to lunch the very next day and we were married six months later on October 1st. He was also exactly the kind of well-bred, well-educated, successful man that my mother might have chosen for me, but I wasn't going to hold that against him—I was smitten. There was a wonderful balance to our relationship. I was the actress, passionate and dramatic, and Steve was thoughtful, practical, and grounded, but still with a great sense of energy and fun. I think it excited him that I was different from all of the other women he had been dating. At the time, he was in his late thirties and newly divorced with two children, and most of the other women he'd been dating were also divorced and had children of their own. I, on the other hand, had never had any children, was making my own money, still had my apartment in the Des Artistes, and I opened a door for him to another way of life. (Although there are pros and cons to marrying an actress: Even now, after thirty-five years of marriage, when he accuses me of being dramatic, I'll say, "Well, you knew what you were getting into." And he smiles—sometimes.)

Early on in our relationship, Steve brought me to an art gallery opening. The gallery belonged to his great friend and college roommate, O. Kelley Anderson, whom I was to meet for the first time. Shortly after we arrived, I was rendered speechless when I spotted a young O. J. Simpson across the room (this was, of course, many years before the infamous glove). Just as I was fumbling for something witty to say to Steve, I heard someone calling my name from afar. I glanced around and saw a shocking head of white hair. It was Andy Warhol, and it turned out that he had recognized me because he was addicted to *Somerset!* Both Steve and Kelley were suitably impressed (as was I, although I acted like it happened every day).

Everything between Steve and me was just so easy. I thought everything he said was brilliant; he thought everything I said was brilliant; I thought his jokes were hilarious; he thought my jokes were hilarious. In short, we just fit with each other.

Of course, like all couples, we had our challenges. Steve's children from his first marriage, Genie and Sandy, were then nine and eleven years old, and the three of us had to learn how to share him. After we were married, like all newlyweds, I wanted to spend as much time with my new husband as possible, but we weren't as free as I would have liked because of Steve's children. They would come and stay with us for the weekend and they were truly terrific kids, but in my mind, they were taking him away from me. You'll hear from any stepmother that this is a very normal thing to feel, but I was jealous of them because, like them, I wanted his time. And we did sort of fight over him—although it seems silly now, especially since I was thirty-two. We would spend wonderful weekends going to the park, or the zoo, or ice skating, or just hanging around the apartment, but when Steve's children left, I had him to myself again—and I just loved that. But I knew that Genie and Sandy loved to be with him alone as well, so sometimes the Good Tina took over and I made plans to go out with my girlfriends when they visited.

As our marriage progressed, we learned to work it out, as couples do. I went to a shrink around that time who gave me some very good advice. She said, "You let him do what he needs to do—see his children, play golf, whatever he wants—and he'll let you do what you need to do." And so, I did. We both gave each other the freedom to follow our own paths. Some people say they'll walk alongside you, but they'll never block your way. And that's what Steve did—whether it was my acting or mothering or traveling with friends—he never blocked my way. He held the string of the kite I was and let me fly, and I always loved coming home to him.

I think that if you are fortunate enough to find a great love, there is nothing quite so marvelous in human existence. There have been few times in my life that I have been as happy as I was in those early days with Steve. The excitement of the chase, the fun of discovering another person, the chemistry that's so strong you can't keep your hands off each other. When those feelings—that spark of romance, the pleasure of falling head over heels, the electrical charge of a first kiss—begin to disappear from our life's script, how do we hold on to them? How do we handle losing that part of ourselves that was once thought of as sexy and desirable—or do we have to? As many of my friends and I have discussed and deliberated, what on earth do we do at this stage in our lives when it comes to men? How do we let go of our Cinderella shoes?

I had a conversation at a party not too long ago with a male friend of mine, someone who, like me, has been happily married for many years. We were watching a young couple who were newly engaged being all lovey-dovey over in the corner and there was something about the adoration and connection between them that pulled the strings of nostalgia in us both. I turned to him and said, "Don't you miss it?" And without even asking what "it" was, he replied, "Oh, yes, I miss it terribly." I don't think there's a person alive over the age of fifty who wouldn't jump at the chance to go back and experience those feelings and the excitement one more time.

Still, I have to be careful that nostalgia doesn't get the best of me. And even though it's easy, especially with the Internet, to look up old beaus and see how they're getting along, I don't see the point of opening the Pandora's Box of past relationships.

I had a beau in college who later went on to become the owner of a major sports franchise. When my son, Renny, was about nine, he became a fan of this team—a fanatic fan. He ate, slept, and breathed for this sport. So I decided to call up my old boyfriend and he invited me to bring Renny and some of his friends to a home game. We arrived at the airport and were met by a limo that whisked us away to a luxury hotel where we were given the entire top floor. The next day, Renny and his friends sat on the playing field while my friend Suzanne and I sat in my old beau's box eating, drinking, laughing, and acting as if we owned the team. Niggling in the back of my mind was the thought, "Hmmm, could all this have been mine?"

These days the thrills I get from interacting with men are both simpler and safer than they were in my younger days. Naturally I got a little rush from the fact that my old beau was giving us such red carpet treatment. Any time I am being acknowledged or doted on by a man, it's hard not to feel a flicker of that old sparkle, that spring in my step. My friend Duane was delighted the other day when she walked by a construction site—yes, the famous construction site—and she heard one of the guys say to his buddies, "An oldie, but a goodie."

My expectations of the men in my life certainly changed as I became an "oldie." What qualifies as a "great date" today is vastly different from what I would have hoped for years ago. Recently

Steve and I were out walking in Central Park, and we wound our way over to the West Side. We reached the park entrance and I turned to Steve and said, "You know, we're over here on the West Side, why don't we have lunch?" So we found a café, someplace we'd never been before, and afterward we were heading home when we passed by a movie theater and decided to go in. He even humored me and let me choose a movie about Coco Chanel. So it was a lovely day, made even more so because it was spontaneous. Not exactly the same out-all-night, bedroom-fireworks kind of date that we would have had when we first met, but it was definitely romantic. I absolutely believe that we can still have real romance as we get older; it's just a calmer, gentler kind.

And this goes for what happens in the bedroom, too. I know a lot of women who have given up on sex altogether because it doesn't feel the same, or they feel self-conscious about their bodies. Not too long ago, I was at lunch with a group of women I'd just met, and when the topic of sex came up, everyone just sat there, staring at their napkins in silence. And I thought, "My God, NO ONE is having any." And a good number of them had wedding rings on. What was wrong with this picture? To be sure, sex for us now is not the same as it was when we were younger and could just fall into bed without any help for him or us. It's both amusing and depressing when we finally realize that the endless stream of Viagra commercials on TV are aimed at us. But I think sex is about life force, pure and simple. We might not be ripping each other's clothes off in the same carefree way that we once did, but it's about saying yes to life, about being close to another person, about going to that place where one forgets and just is.

Of course I have a good number of women friends of a "certain age" who are happily single and have no real desire, physical or otherwise, to get involved with a man at this stage. Most are widowed or divorced, and even if they would like to find someone to do things with, they feel like it is too much work to get out there again, or they fear becoming a "nurse or a purse." Some of them even feel as though they have come into their own during this stage, especially the ones who married young, and they are now enjoying their independence. But I think that most of us, no matter how independent we are, also enjoy companionship and its creature comforts. After Steve and I come home from a party, we'll talk about it, and share our observations about the night, and that is a wonderful thing. If you don't have to worry about money and have plenty of girlfriends, then men may not be necessary for you. You don't need them to take you out to dinner; you can take yourself out to dinner. And if sex no longer matters to you, then you don't need them for that. But I do think they give us something that we can't give ourselves. It's that "Cinderella" feeling, that sparkle that lights us up from the inside and, perhaps more than anything else, gives us back our youthful glow.

My friend Duane became a widow ten years ago (if you say she "lost" her husband, she'll retort, "Did I leave him somewhere?") and it took her several years to start dating again. "Did you know that widows used to be called relics?" she informed me. "And in some parts of India, if you're a widow, they still shave your head and send you to the equivalent of a nunnery. That is, if you haven't jumped on the funeral pyre." She was contemplating becoming involved with someone new and trying to decide whether or not she was ready. She finally reasoned, "Well, I'm not in India, and my life's not over. The least I can do is try to enjoy myself."

The first man she went out with was a jazz enthusiast who was always taking her to jazz clubs. Duane knew nothing about jazz and had never particularly liked it, but she went along for the ride because she did like the guy. "At one point," she told me, after their third or fourth date, "I just thought to myself, 'I'm feigning interest as fast as I can.' You know, like the old expression 'I'm dancing as fast as I can.' I'm not sure how much more jazz I can take!"

They dated for a while longer, and ultimately parted ways. But Duane did admit after the fact that she had learned something about music and that it had been kind of neat (a word right out of the fifties) to do something she would never have done with her husband. "I think dating is really about new opportunities," she concluded. "If you can approach it that way and not get hung up on the what-ifs or the strangeness of kissing someone new, it can be fun."

My friend Jean, however, wasn't so sure after her first brush with dating after her husband died. "He was a perfectly lovely man," she said. "We went to the theater, but I'm telling you, I could not wait to get out of that car! I think the car was still moving and my feet were on the street before we even got to my building. My doorman met us at the curb and opened the car door and I was just thinking, 'Thank God.' I wasn't ready. It made me think of that famous line from Gloria Steinem: 'A woman needs a man like a fish needs a bicycle.' These days I feel like that fish. I don't know if I'll ever be ready. I've got a lot of other parts of my life to focus on right now. And that's fine."

Of course, for many women, dating at this time in our lives can be fun, IF you find the right man, which as we all know, is always the challenge. And at our age, you have to get a bit creative. There is always the strategy of being the first person to bring a casserole to the man who is newly divorced or widowed, and I actually know several very happy marriages that have happened this way. Married men often can't take care of themselves when they are suddenly left alone and many end up practically stranded in their own homes, living off cans of Chef Boyardee. There are plenty of places you can meet the right man, such as parties, the theater, or even high school or college reunions (always good as they will most likely remember you as the adorable cheerleader you once were).

But a lot of my friends scoff at these suggestions—they sound great in theory, and you always hear the stories about the woman who met her second husband while she was getting her windshield wipers fixed or some such thing, but finding someone new can be really difficult. "Everyone always says that you can meet someone on a plane," my friend Jill, a fashion designer who has been divorced for fifteen years, was telling me. "Well, I've never met anyone on a plane—not once! And I travel for work all the time."

And of course, you can always rely on the efforts of "concerned" friends and family who think you really, really, really need to meet someone (funny how this also happens in our twenties). My friend Nancy's family was determined to see her happy, so they hatched a scheme to get her out and dating again. One summer evening, her son had a group of friends over for a barbeque and they were all milling around outside in the garden. Nancy went inside to grab something from the kitchen and happened to notice two of the girls hunched over the computer in the study. "What are you girls doing?" she asked. And they answered, "Oh, we've just signed you up for eHarmony!"

"Oh no, I don't do that," Nancy resisted. But her son and his friends were adamant. So the next day, against her better judgment, she logged on to see what kind of responses she had received. "I don't know what they put in that computer," she told me, "but I wound up with an electrician in Pennsylvania, a plumber in Connecticut . . . I mean, I do work with contractors, but these people weren't even in Manhattan! I'm not driving for hours just for some blind date. I can have a bad blind date in New York just as well and save money on tolls."

A few weeks later, a friend called her up and said, "Nancy, I've got the perfect person for you. I'm giving a dinner at Twenty-one in the wine cellar downstairs. It will be small, twenty people, and I'd love to introduce you." So Nancy went to the dinner and her friend immediately corralled her. "I'm so glad you're here. Come and let me introduce you to Harvey."

"She led me over to this man," Nancy related to me the next day, "and when he turned around I thought I was looking at Teddy Roosevelt. He had the mustache. He had the glasses. He was even wearing a three-piece suit with a little gold chain! And to top it off, he looked about eighty years old. I said to my friend a little later on, 'What were you thinking?' and she sniffed, 'Well, he's a very interesting man. He lives in Japan for part of the year.' And I told her, 'Well, he may be very interesting, but he's definitely not for me.'"

But the truly great thing about women dating at our age is that, unlike in their younger days, most are not willing to compromise.

I always love hearing the dating stories of my single friends because it's a chance for me to share in the possibilities of new romance vicariously. But the truly great thing about women dating at our age is that, unlike in their younger days, most are not willing to compromise. My friend Trudy ended a relationship with an otherwise promising man she'd met on vacation with her girlfriends in Napa Valley because it was long distance and she felt like she was spending all her free time traveling to see him. "He didn't like Los Angeles," she recalled. "He thought it was too flashy, too trendy for him. And he couldn't understand why I didn't think his hometown in northern California was just as great as my own. And then I started giving up stuff. My friends would invite me to go out to dinner or do other things and I would have to decline because I was always out of town. I started making choices that took me away from things I enjoy and I thought, 'No, no, no, I can't do this. This is not a good place to be.' So I ended it. It was hard because on the outside, he was perfect. The package looked good. But I also really like the life I've built for myself. I couldn't give it up."

My friend Paula agrees: "One thing I've learned how to do since my husband died is to enjoy the pleasures of being *with* myself as opposed to *by* myself. I have a lot more space to do the things that are important to me and to develop my own interests, and I've come to really relish that." And then she laughs. "I do want love and companionship—just not twenty-four/seven!"

It's true that getting back into the world of dating at our age can be a bumpy experience if you've been out of the game for a while. My friend Alina's children, unbeknownst to her, signed her up for online dating, too, with similarly hilarious and disastrous results. She had recently moved from Miami to New York and her son had written up the profile for her. But he'd clicked the box that said Alina would go out with "any guy from age twenty-five to fifty-five"—even as he also noted that she was a "grandmother who loves spending time with her grandchildren." "You should have seen who was in my inbox," she said. "I only checked it once and then never again. I mean, I really don't think online dating is a bad idea in theory, but people lie. Some of these men who e-mailed me—I just knew they were lying about their age. And who wants that? Plus, if I tell the truth and say I'm sixty-four, no one will believe me and they'll automatically think I'm older. And most men out there already want to date younger women anyway."

Some of the single women I know are reluctant to begin dating because they fear being compared with younger women, especially when the lights go out. I myself am not particularly modest, and I've always believed that I am who I am, but I'm not typical in this sense; I think most women my age are a little nervous about taking their clothes off with someone new. We look at our softening bodies and think, "How could he possibly find me attractive?" But I don't think men see our flaws as much as we do. If they are taking the time to court you and buy you dinner, it is you with all your flaws they want. If they are solely interested in bedding a woman for her body, they'll go for someone who's twenty or thirty. Or they'll pay. And either way, those men are not likely to be good company down the road.

But the idea that May-December romances can only go one way, with the older man pursuing the young, nubile twenty-something, is a myth. In fact, I know several women who have been surprised by a much younger suitor in this phase of life. And let me tell you, from the looks on their faces, nothing will give you a jolt of youth and vitality like a heady love affair with a younger man.

My friend Alina—remember, she is sixty-four—was sitting in a restaurant having dinner with a friend when a man who looked no more than thirty sidled up to them. He was quite good-looking, tall, and well-dressed in an impeccably tailored, expensive suit, and Alina had noticed him eyeing their table from the bar.

"Do I know you?" he asked. He completely ignored the friend, his gaze was fixed solely on Alina.

"I don't think so," she said.

"Are you Brazilian?"

"No." Alina is Cuban, so she has that Latin look about her, but she has lived in the United States since she was a teenager.

"Because I lived in São Paulo, and I thought maybe I knew you there."

"No."

And then he said, "Would you mind if I called you for a drink?"

Alina started laughing and looked at her friend, and then back at this young man. "No, that would be very nice." He gave her his business card and they exchanged a few more pleasantries and then the young man left them to their dinner.

Alina turned to her friend and said, "Margarita, I promise you that this doesn't happen to me. I promise you. This is like once in forty years!"

She went home that night with his business card, thinking, "What should I do with this?" She thought it over for a few days and then decided to send him an e-mail. She wrote, "I was very flattered the other night that you came over to talk to me, so yes, I'd love to get together for a drink."

"I was dying," she told me later, "because I'd never done anything like this in my whole life! But he e-mailed right back and said, 'Yes, I'd love to get together. I'll be in Europe next week, but let's do it when I get back. And by the way, you look gorgeous in black.'"

Well, Alina was beside herself. "But then," she told me a few weeks later, "I never heard from him again." She laughed. "I'm sure that the very next morning, he Googled me and my whole life history came up. He probably realized just how old I am. And that's fine—I mean, it's completely normal that he wouldn't call me. You know, my first instinct was to e-mail him and say, 'I'm very flattered, but I'm much too old for you.' But then I thought, let me play with this a little bit and see what happens. And I think that's good. I'm glad I did."

Even if it doesn't evolve into anything, the thrill we get from that kind of flirtation alone can give you a terrific lift. When my friend Clarice was visiting Paris with her twenty-eight-year-old daughter, a friend back home had suggested they meet up with someone he knew—a young, successful Frenchman whom he thought would be perfect for the daughter. So they called up this fellow and arranged to meet for a drink at a little café on the Rue de Rivoli. But when they all sat down together, he began showering his attentions on Clarice! "It was so funny," she recalls. "I mean, I wasn't liking it that my daughter was being passed over for me, but it was definitely flattering. It was an empowering moment. It's nice to realize that you can still be looked at like that, to be the one who's drawing the focus. It was sort of a funny feeling, because he was so young—a kid, really. But he was French! Somehow that made it all okay."

And sometimes, these flirtations do lead to something more. My friend Alina did wind up becoming involved with a much younger man—an artist from Cuba who shared her cultural heritage and swept her off her feet. "It was totally unexpected," she recalls. "But he really brought me back to life after my husband died. I figured, 'If I want to have a good time, that's okay.' He gave me a reason to get up in the morning. He also introduced me to a whole new world of contemporary art that I still enjoy today even though we are no longer together. And because he was an artist and very conscious of beauty, I started dressing a little prettier, a little sexier, for him. I still have a pair of red high heels that I bought during that time and that I still wear for going out, and every time I put them on I feel sexy. It's wonderful to feel that way again."

Even if you are married, you can still enjoy the attentions of a younger man from time to time. When I was on *Guiding Light*, there was a darling boy who briefly played my granddaughter's husband (of course it was brief, we're talking about a soap opera). Even though he was considerably younger than me, he flirted with me mercilessly (and everyone else) and would even sometimes pat my bottom. While some women would no doubt object to this kind of attention at work, I loved it! He was treating me as though I were his age and every bit as attractive as all the younger actresses running around. And I wasn't.

I knew a woman very well who fell in love with a man when she was in her seventies and swore up and down that it was the best sex she ever had. She confessed that she and her lover would often sneak off to be alone, away from the children and grandchildren, who were always around. When she told me this story, I was in my forties and horrified, but now that I'm in my sixties I see how marvelous this was. She was living proof that passion and romance are not only for the young (despite what the advertisers want us to believe).

These days I try to keep the spark alive—in my marriage to Steve, but also within myself. I don't want to lose the part of me that had so much fun falling in love and being pursued so many, many, many years ago. I think, more than anything, feeling sexy and desirable is about energy. It's about tapping that flirtatious instinct that all women have—even if it's been dormant for a while—that can make a man smile and encourage him to do the same for you.

Alina, being Cuban, is an expert at this kind of flirtation, as so many Latins are. She's used to that playful banter back and forth because it's part of her culture. "When I'm in Miami," she says, "the gardener flirts with me, the man fixing my car . . . everybody flirts! And you don't get that every day. But it makes you feel good. It doesn't go anywhere, but that kind of interaction makes life a lot more fun."

I think, above all, that flirting is really about playfulness, and this sense of playfulness is what keeps us young. The other day I chatted playfully with the man who was fixing my orthotics, of all things. And of course husbands love to be flirted with, too, especially when you let them know that you find them just as attractive as you did when you were first married and bouncing into bed every minute of the day. While it's true that men don't fret about their aging bodies as much as we do, and they certainly spend less time trying to fight back, I guarantee you that your husband misses his hair and the fact that he used to have abs he could actually see. Bringing back that playfulness, that suggestive banter, to your relationship can make both of you feel youthful once again.

> *I think, more than anything, feeling sexy and desirable is about energy. It's about tapping that flirtatious instinct that all women have.*

It's also fun to mix things up and get outside your normal routine. A friend who is into all those "trendy New Age things" once suggested to me that Steve and I change the sides that we sleep on in bed. For thirty years, I'd been on the left and he'd been on the right. Luckily, Steve humored me (he's good-natured enough to allow me my moments of insanity). That night when he came home, I'd moved all of his things to my side and vice versa. And he got out of bed two days later and started his own firm, something he'd been talking about doing for ten years! (It's been five years since this happened . . . maybe it's time to switch sides again, or move the bed altogether. Who knows what might transpire?)

Fortunately, there are lots of other tricks we can use as well that don't involve rearranging the furniture. When I was in my fifties, I was lucky enough to visit my very smart gynecologist who asked me straight up about my sex life. All I could do at first was stare at her blankly. At the time, I was in the midst of caring for my aging parents and sex was the absolute last thing on my mind. This bothered me, but I was so tired and overwhelmed all the time that I just chalked it up to the familiarity of a twenty-odd-year marriage and getting older. It didn't occur to me to do anything about it, because I didn't know that I could. I missed sex but had concluded that maybe it just wasn't supposed to be a part of this stage in our lives.

But this doctor told me that much of the change in sex drive that we women experience as we age has nothing to do with us or our partner, and everything to do with hormones. And here's the truth, straight from Lillian the Nurse: Estrogen and testosterone will MAKE you interested in sex. My doctor prescribed both and I couldn't believe how they lifted my mood. Within a matter of days, all the old impulses came roaring back. I felt young and sexy and aware, and well . . . frisky. So medical science has come to our rescue once again, much in the same way it did in the late sixties when birth control became readily available. Believe me, I'm convinced that in the old days, no one ever did it after the age of sixty. But today there are lots of nifty things to try like fancy lubricants or Vagifem (a great little pill that keeps you moist) that can jump-start our libido and keep us frisky as we age. If you need a little inspiration, just watch Judi Dench in the British sitcom *As Time Goes By*, or Diane Keaton and Jack Nicholson in *Something's Gotta Give* (of course Diane Keaton is thin and perfect, so we all hate her).

But as we all know, cultivating romance and recapturing that Cinderella feeling are about more than just sex. So much of what enables us to enjoy both these things stems from maintaining a strong connection with your partner. Over the course of our marriage, like all couples, Steve and I have been pulled away from each other from time to time. We both worked, and we had our son, Renny, to raise, as well as visits from Steve's two children, and there were plenty of days when the only time we came together was when we were lying down next to each other to go to sleep at night. For a while, Renny took all of my attention, and Steve minded. Sometimes his business pulled him away, and I minded. But we were lucky in that we were both able to give each other space, and were old enough and had seen enough of relationships that we had no ridiculous thoughts of perfection in the other person.

One thing we did try to do on a regular basis was to take a trip together and go away to a place where we could have an adventure, just the two of us. We had some crazy experiences, but they made for good stories and brought us closer together. One time we were taking the Red Train in Russia from Moscow to St. Petersburg, and our guide warned us that we should put a cork in the door to our compartment. Otherwise bandits would try to gas us through the keyhole and then steal all our belongings. Steve loves trains so he had thought it would be a grand and romantic idea to take this overnight train together, but we spent most of that night scared stiff while the train clattered through the Russian countryside. I can still see him bending over, trying to wedge that cork into the lock. Not exactly the romantic getaway he had envisioned!

Now that we are older—he is seventy-three and I am sixty-seven—and it's just the two of us again, spending time together is easier, but it still takes work. You have to be careful not to let complacency take over. A few summers ago, we were invited to a wedding in Sun Valley, Idaho, a gorgeous place surrounded by mountains. We were making our plans and Steve suggested that we do something we'd never done before: take a road trip. So after the wedding, we rented a car and drove the 470 miles from Sun Valley to see friends in Bend, Oregon. We had a great time stopping at all the small towns along the way, staying in local inns, and trying to navigate the winding mountain roads. At one point, Steve turned to me and said, "I had forgotten what you were like!" Here we'd been sleeping in the same bed for years and we'd both lost sight of the person we married.

Now, instead of resisting life's slowing down, we try to take advantage of our more relaxed schedules to make sure that we spend time together. We still give each other our independence—he loves his golf as much as ever, and I still love a night out with my soap actor friends, which isn't necessarily Steve's thing. But when given the chance, Steve can be very romantic. When we decide to do something, he's meticulous about planning it so that we have the best seats, the best table, the perfect spot to grab a hot chocolate after the movie. But women can be the planners, too. We need to give ourselves the opportunity to put on our Cinderella shoes and feel like we're being courted again.

Someone asked me recently if I would ever consider getting remarried again if something happened to Steve. But because I've been so spoiled with him—he gives me such immense freedom and such immense care—I think that I probably would not. But many of my friends say they would remarry because at the end of the day, they really cherish that kind of companionship. And I know what they mean. It's not that I have to go and sit in the den every time that Steve's watching baseball or football, or that we have wild and crazy sex every night, or that I don't think I could handle things on my own. I know that I could. It's just that he's there, and I'm here, sitting in another room reading, and maybe I'll trot in and say hi and kiss him and then get back to my book. It's just having that person. It's seeing another coffee cup in the sink next to your own.

It might not be quite as juicy or explosive as it was years ago (although who's to say that it can't be if you set your mind to it?), but there's a sweetness to love and romance that comes in this phase of life. We can't give up on it. It's there. The pain comes without looking for it, so put on your Cinderella shoes and find a ball to go to. When we have an opportunity for joy, as we do with the men in our lives—whether they're a handsome stranger in the market or a husband waiting for us at home—we need to seize it, treasure it, and make it happen. We need to remain forever frisky.

Hormones: The Lowdown

I've had a very good experience with estrogen and testosterone, but every woman needs to decide with her doctor if taking hormones is right for her. There are negatives to it, including an increased risk of breast cancer, so you will have to make up your own mind as to whether it's worth it. For me it was, as the pain of the blahs was so great.

Today I take estrogen, which comes in a patch that I change once a week. I've found it to be a great mood elevator. And the testosterone comes as a gel that you apply to your wrists at night. Testosterone is what brings back the sexual impulses you had when you were younger (and no, it won't give you a mustache). Any woman over sixty who has no desire can recapture it just by visiting the doctor and asking a few difficult questions. And if your doctor doesn't bring it up, do it yourself—or change doctors.

I had a single friend who always said that she wanted to meet someone, but would walk by incredibly handsome and available men who were holding the door for her or waiting on line for a table at a restaurant, without giving them so much as a glance. I would mention this to her and she was totally oblivious. So I wondered if this might be due to a lack of the hormones that once made her feel sexy and attuned to the men around her. I told her about my experience and recommended that she talk to her doctor, and after a few weeks on testosterone the change in her was apparent. Suddenly she began noticing the men around her and soon she was meeting men and going on dates. Now when we are in a restaurant or at a party I will ask her how many men are there. And she usually knows, because she has regained that awareness, of both the men who cross her path and the fact that she is still a woman.

CHAPTER FOUR

Make Something Important

One day in 1983, several years after my son, Renny, was born, I got a call from Gail Kobe, the executive producer on *Guiding Light*. She said, "Tina, I don't know how you'd feel about playing the mother of a twenty-year-old." How would I feel? ECSTATIC! I wouldn't have cared if they'd asked me to play the mother of an eighty-year-old, even though I was only forty at the time.

They wanted me for the role of Lillian Raines, a new character on the show who was going to be coping with a physically abusive husband. It was only a six-month story line, but the role had lots of opportunity for high emotions and drama. What could be better? *Guiding Light* boasted more than ten million viewers worldwide every day and had the distinction of being America's longest-running soap opera (it had originally debuted as *The Guiding Light* on radio in 1937). There were plenty of actresses my age who would have turned down a role in which they'd be playing a twenty-year-old's mother, but I had no problem with it: I couldn't wait to start being Lillian.

I got the part, Gail told me, because she liked the idea of hiring a strong woman to play a weak one. "Watching a weak woman play another weak woman is boring," she said. "Having you in this role is going to be far more exciting."

Lillian's story line turned out to be a sensation. Her character was the polar opposite of me, which made playing her a challenge, but that was part of the fun. I had to keep Edith Bunker in my mind as a model, particularly the way she dressed and always ran to do everything that Archie Bunker wanted on the show *All in the Family*. Lillian's husband, Bradley Raines, was an abusive monster who beat her and belittled her on a daily basis. He'd say, "Shut up, Lillian! It's all your fault. Get me a beer." And I'd say, "Yes, Bradley," and run off to the kitchen. I'd come hurrying back with the bottle, and I'd even have opened it for him, just like a servant girl, because I was so desperate to keep him happy. I didn't want him to get angry and hit me or my daughter, Beth. We used that line about beer so many times that to this day, whenever I get together with Grant Aleksander, Michael O'Leary, Krista Tesreau, Judi Evans, and James Rebhorn (who played Phillip Spaulding; Dr. Rick Bauer; Mindy Lewis; my daughter, Beth; and Bradley Raines respectively), we look at one another and say, "Shut up, Lillian! Get me a beer." And then we all burst out laughing.

The story line really captured viewers' attention, even more so when it was revealed that in addition to all the bruises and black eyes, Bradley had gone so far as to rape Beth. This was the first time that incest and sexual abuse had ever been dealt with on television and our ratings went through the roof. We suddenly had twelve million people watching us, and became the number one soap. As we approached the end of my six-month contract, the producer who had hired me warned me, "Tina, you cannot save this character." "I'm not trying to save her," I replied. But of course I was—I loved playing her and wanted to continue to do so.

The story culminated in an elaborate trial that ultimately sent Bradley to prison. Originally, the writers had planned for Lillian to fly off the handle and kill him after she learned about the rape, but when I found this out I went straight to the powers that be and convinced them that we needed to be extremely sensitive and responsible with this story line. Over the past few weeks, we'd been flooded with hundreds of heartbreaking letters from girls who were in the same situation as Beth, and we didn't want them to think that murdering their abuser was the answer.

"If I kill him and go to jail," I told them, "then Beth will be left alone, and all the young girls going through the same thing out there won't go to their mothers because they'll be terrified of losing both parents." The producers heard me, and instead Lillian and Beth went to rape crisis centers and courts and put Bradley in prison, and in the end, they decided to keep me around! I was thrilled, and that proved to be the start of the most wonderful twenty-six years of my career. And it was only the beginning for Lillian.

Set in the fictional town of Springfield (there is one in every state, and this one seemed to be somewhere near Chicago), *Guiding Light* followed the lives and deaths, loves and marriages, and hatreds and vendettas of five families: the wealthy Spauldings (my daughter, Beth, married two of them), the downscale Coopers (I married one of them), the even more downscale Shaynes, and the stable, upper-middle-class Lewises and Bauers. The story was originally about the Bauers as they had been in Springfield since the beginning. Ed Bauer and his son Rick were both doctors at Cedars Hospital, so Lillian spent a lot of time with them and even had an affair with Ed (while, later on, Beth had an affair with his son Rick. And when I fell in love with Buzz Cooper, Beth fell in love with his son Coop. We were a good mother-daughter team.). Beth was married many, many times and had many, many more love affairs than her mother could have dreamed of. Reva Shayne, played by Kim Zimmer, was a poor girl who came to town and proceeded to marry Josh Lewis . . . and then his dad, and then his brother. Her character was wild and exciting and people loved her; she became one of the true anchors of the show. But we all had our moments of glory when the story line we were shooting was the one that kept the fans glued to their television sets. The writers on the show were just amazing—you never knew what outrageous plot twists they were going to come up with next.

Even Lillian, who was supposedly sweet and cowering, managed to have her fair share of jaw-dropping story lines, which made going to work every day delicious fun. After Bradley went to jail for raping Beth, Beth disappeared, leaving one red shoe by a lake. She came back to life, was in a fire, and became blind and aphasic, meaning she didn't understand anyone or anything (really convenient on a soap opera). I caused my best friend Maureen's death after I slept with her husband, Ed Bauer, the doctor who was helping me through a bout of breast cancer. Maureen found out and drove off a snowy cliff in a moment of distraction and the fans were positively livid—many of them never forgave me. *I* never forgave me. I killed someone by mistake, Beth killed someone who was stalking her, and my seven-year-old granddaughter— SEVEN YEARS OLD—killed a man who was abusing her mother. Quite a set of genes we all had. Then Beth drowned in the lake—again—and left another red shoe behind. She returned from the dead—again—but this time as a completely different woman named Lorelei who looked exactly the same, and yet I didn't recognize her. Then I DID recognize her. Beth's daughter, my granddaughter (played by Hayden Panettiere, now famous for her role on *Heroes*), got lymphoma but lived through a cord-blood transplant from her newborn brother who had the same father as she did, but shouldn't have, as Beth was now married to a different person. I got engaged to Hawk Shayne who left me for his ex-wife, and then I dated all sorts of men before finally moving into the Spaulding mansion where I could take care of my grandchildren (while their grandfather on their father's side proceeded to murder their father and marry their mother—very *Hamlet*). Eventually I found a boyfriend named Buzz and no longer felt like taking care of everyone else.

Can you see why I loved my job?

Every morning, I'd get up and arrive at the rehearsal hall at seven. We would all gather around, perusing our scripts, at times screaming with laughter over the lines we were going to say that day. People like Grant Aleksander (Phillip Spaulding), Ron Raines (Alan Spaulding), Jordan Clarke (Billy Lewis), and Justin Deas (Buzz Cooper) would keep us laughing all day long with their comic asides and witticisms. The scripts for the week—we shot one episode a day—would arrive the Friday before so you could learn your lines over the weekend. Each script was about seventy pages long, which was a lot of material to learn if you happened to be in a major story line—there were times when a few actors would have almost the entire script and this could go on for months and months. You have to be very smart to be successful on soaps. There is a tremendous amount of material that has to be produced every day, and the pace of shooting is so relentless that you have to be really sharp to stay on top of it and do it well. And we almost never got multiple takes because there just wasn't time; you had to nail the scene on the first try, which was why those early morning rehearsals were so important.

During rehearsal, some of the actors would get grumpy (after all, it was only seven A.M.) if the rest of us were talking too loudly. But usually everyone was chatting and having a great time and scarfing down the cereal and fruit and coffee that craft services had put out for us. We'd take turns stepping into the open space to do our scenes and calling up the tensions and emotions we'd need to produce during the actual filming later on. The directors gave us feedback so we'd all be on the same page when we arrived on set.

Rehearsal went from seven to nine, and by nine you had to be camera-ready if your scene was up first. So after you'd rehearsed, you'd go to hair and makeup and have the stylists work their magic. When I first arrived on the show, I learned the importance of being ready on time from a terrific actress named Beverlee McKinsey, who played Alexandra Spaulding (a role also played by Joan Collins and most recently by Marj Dusay). Beverlee was one of the greatest soap actresses ever, and her character, Alexandra, was a linchpin of the show. But as important as she was, she always arrived on set early, before anyone else, and had her makeup and hair done by the time the rest of us got there. She was the model of a star who was never a diva, and she set an exemplary tone for the rest of us.

After hair and makeup, we'd head over to wardrobe to get our clothes for that day. When I first came on the show, we had lots of money, so our clothes came from places like Bergdorf Goodman and Saks Fifth Avenue—we would go to the stores for fittings in these beautiful, elegant designer clothes and shoes. There were some clothes, especially the gowns that we wore for party scenes (and the Spauldings were always throwing parties) that were just thrilling to wear. Occasionally an actor would argue about what they were wearing with the costume designer. But for the most part, people were happy with what they wore, and we could always borrow the clothes for use outside the show, which was a lifesaver if you hated to shop. Playing a nurse, I was usually in my white nurse's uniform, which was fun, but let's face it—nowhere near as fun as those gorgeous designer outfits (although definitely better than what I wore in my hospital scenes in later years—I don't imagine that many men have fantasies about nurses anymore now that they've given up those short white skirts for scrubs).

It was also the costume designer on *Guiding Light* who gave me one of my all-time favorite pairs of shoes: the white Chanel high heels that went with my nurse's uniform. They were sleek and simple and very pretty—and it didn't hurt that they were Chanel. Whenever I put them on, I always got a little rush because I was about to go in front of the cameras and do a scene. In a way, they were an extension of the black Chanel heels I had worn to all my auditions back in the early days, but while those shoes were all about possibility, these were about success. I was now an established working actress, and there is no word more wonderful to an actress than *working*. And I was on a show I loved with people I adored. Rather heavenly.

After we were dressed and ready to go, we'd wait in our dressing rooms, gossiping or running lines until we were called to the set over the loudspeaker. On any given day, you might have only one scene—or many if your character was currently involved in a major story line. And you might be in the first scene as well as the last, which could make for a very long day. The scenes were filmed completely out of order from how they would ultimately appear on the show, especially in the days before we had permanent sets.

If I was taking someone to the hospital who'd been poisoned in the Spaulding study, I might tape the hospital scene first, and then the poisoning-in-the-Spaulding-study scene a few days later. This was disconcerting, as we might forget how we had felt during the hospital scene, but we all became very adept at this kind of switching around—although there were definitely times when the emotional continuity was lost.

The costume continuity was off at times, too. I was watching the show one day on TV and smiled when I saw myself walk into a patient's room wearing my uniform and a pink sweater, and then when we cut to the interior of the room in the next scene, I was in street clothes. And then in the next scene I came out of the room in the uniform with the pink sweater again. HILARIOUS! The interior scene had been shot a week after the exterior scenes, and somehow we all forgot that I had been wearing my nurse's uniform. And somehow this mix-up had made it into the air show.

But all of us had an incredible time in our roles, and couldn't believe the things we got to do every day. Beth was forever getting involved with rich, bad men, even though, as Lillian, I was always "suggesting" to her that she be a good person and not get involved with whatever rich, bad man she was currently seeing (although I don't know why, as I usually got to go and live with her in their splendid houses with servants to wait on us and cooks to make us dinner). One time she fell in love with a Prince who inexplicably came to Springfield and we all went away with him to his island in the Caribbean, where Beth married him and became a princess and I was suddenly ROYALTY. We got to wear glorious clothes and have balls in our honor and Lillian was swept off her feet by a painter who said, "I can either paint you or make love to you." I mean, really. Even so, I was still urging Beth to not marry the Prince, but go home and remarry her former husband, Phillip

Spaulding. Sadly, we had to leave the island after the Prince locked Beth in a tower and tried to kill her. It turned out that he was a murderer and had been murdering people all over Springfield. And after Beth had escaped, she said, "Mom, you were right." Just as she always did. Until the next time.

Some of the stories were so over the top they were actually very difficult to play. When Beth came back from the dead after having drowned for the second time, I supposedly didn't recognize her even though everything about her, from her hair to her voice to the mole on her chest, was EXACTLY the same. And yet, I was supposed to be treating her as this completely new person named Lorelei. I just kept looking at our writers and saying, "Guys, I'm sorry, but I'm her MOTHER. You're going to have to tell me again how it is that I don't recognize my own child." And I wasn't trying to be difficult, I just couldn't wrap my head around how this was remotely plausible. I said, "I'm looking at her and she looks exactly the same." And they would say, "You just don't." This went on for about six months during which I was with Beth/Lorelei all the time, and Phillip Spaulding, her former husband, would look at me and say, "Doesn't she remind you of someone?" and I'd say, "Yes." We'd both be about to break down and laugh, and I'd be biting my tongue, and Phillip would turn around as we couldn't even look at each other without smiling. And then one day I DID recognize her and she went back to being Beth again. It was absolutely insane.

Then there were times when I was the insane one. One of these involved a party scene in which—since I happened to be there and I was a nurse—I was supposed to pronounce someone dead. We were all at the Spaulding mansion, dressed to the nines and drinking champagne, when the doorbell rang. The butler answered the door and this character, Carl, was standing there, covered head to toe in mud. The script called for Carl to pitch forward onto the floor, and I was supposed to run over to him, check his pulse, and say, "His eyes are fixed and dilated. He has no pulse. He is dead!"

Now, I HATE, DETEST, HATE certain smells and can always smell anything way ahead of anyone else: smoke from a cigarette miles away; smoke on the clothes of someone who was smoking hours before; paint fumes; fish; perfume; nail polish; laundry detergent . . . you name it. I get headaches instantly, and they wouldn't even call me into work on the days when there was going to be a fire—like a car exploding—because I would get really sick from the fumes. I never use hair spray and once when my yoga teacher started washing her clothes in Tide I had to change yoga teachers. This was all taken for granted at the studio, and they really tried to accommodate me, as I had been there for so long and never complained about anything EXCEPT smells.

So on that day, when Carl's slime-covered body fell through the door—supposedly because he had fallen in a swamp after he was shot—I was standing at the top of the staircase about to run down and check his pulse, and then . . . I stopped. Because Carl just REEKED. I don't know what kind of mud they'd covered him in, but they must have gotten it from some greenhouse supply with manure in it, because it stunk to high heaven. I didn't know what to do, but I knew that if I got any closer to him I would throw up. The cameras were rolling, and remember—one take. So from my perch on the top of the stairs, as far away from the body as I could possibly be, I yelled out my lines: "He's dead! He has no pulse and his eyes are fixed and dilated!"

Of course, I was on a staircase and nowhere near the body and there was no way I could have possibly seen his eyes—but everyone in the room knew exactly why I was staying there: because this was the FOULEST SMELL IN THE WORLD. The poor actor who played Carl—what a trouper he was—just lay there on the floor like a dead fish. Fortunately, when the director came out to ask what I was doing on the staircase, he was overtaken by the stench and didn't even try to suggest a retake.

There were plenty of other amusing moments, too, as we tried to make these characters and their stories come to life. Sets would fall over and we'd just keep going. Or someone would walk into a closet thinking it was actually the exit and then would just stay there, hoping nobody would notice. Often we would get the laughter out in rehearsals. We'd crack our jokes and make fun of one another, but then we totally committed to doing whatever it was we had to do. Sometimes it would be a breeze and sometimes it was really difficult. One time Beth, completely out of the blue, locked Ron Raines and Ricky Paull Goldin in a cabin and started beating them with baseball bats. We were all reading the script and thinking, "What on earth?" Or the time—in one of the show's more infamous plot twists—that Kim Zimmer's character, Reva, was cloned. Her clone went from infancy to adulthood in a matter of weeks and was supposed to save her life in some way. Kim had to play both Reva and this clone, and we'd all be laughing at the absurdity of the story, and she'd say between guffaws, "Look, I've gotta play it, stop it." And she was right. But we'd be rolling our eyes.

We had plenty of laughs at the hospital, too. We nicknamed Michael O'Leary, who played Dr. Rick Bauer, "Dr. Death" because his character killed thirty-nine people over the course of the show. Thirty-nine! And not because he was killing them on purpose; he was just a terrible doctor. If your character was going to him for an operation and your contract was up for renegotiation you knew you were in trouble. After he'd "killed" twenty-three patients on air, we brought out a cake as he now held the record for most TV deaths. And yet, this was the same character who, years before, had gone to medical school for SIX MONTHS and emerged—you guessed it—a "brilliant" physician.

Years ago, when *ER* first came on the air, *Guiding Light* decided to emulate their more realistic approach, so they asked Dr. Rick and me to do a complete operation. The detailed medical scenes and complicated terminology were supposed to flow from us like it was second nature. But Mikey, as we all called him, and I both had a problem with the "big" words of the medical world. We worked on this operation scene for days and spent hours rehearsing, but Dr. Rick still ordered a C-SPAN rather than a C-section and I passed him a spatula, not a scalpel. Yet somehow we pulled it off. That's the incredible thing about playing a character on a soap: sometimes you're smart and sometimes you're not, and you never know which it's going to be until you see the day's script. One day you'll be smart enough to piece together a murder mystery and the next you won't even recognize your own daughter.

But there were also the really powerful moments, when we delivered beautifully written, heart-wrenching lines. When I had the affair with Dr. Ed Bauer, his wife, Maureen, found out and confronted me. I was her best friend, and she looked me in the eye and said, "You made us into a suburban cliché." What a perfect line. And there was the time, after Beth's husband Jim was killed in a fire, that she came to me and burst into tears and said, "I just got in the car, and the seat was pushed way back the way he liked it." It just broke your heart. We liked to laugh about the silly stories, but the truth about soaps is that you do go through death and life and love and hate in a very real way. And most of the time it's just wonderfully done.

During my years on the show, I had several story lines that really made an impact. Maureen's death haunted the show until the end. But the story I was most proud of was the one in which Lillian had breast cancer. This was the first time that breast cancer had been dealt with on daytime television, and the story went on for about a year and helped millions of women by raising awareness. We did the story as a tribute to one of our producers, Kathy Chambers, who had died from breast cancer. The writers actually had me find the lump on camera while I sat at my dressing table after a shower, and the story followed me through the diagnosis and treatment: mammogram, sonogram, biopsy, removal of the cancer, radiation, and support group therapy. It was all done with realism and dignity, and there were some raw, gut-wrenching lines that gave voice to what women with this disease go through. I said to Ed Bauer, my confidant and a doctor, "I've seen women who have lost their breasts and I've consoled them. But now it's happening to me. Will a man ever look at me again? Will anyone ever want to sleep with me again?"

After each show, I would appear in a public service announcement and urge women to check for breast cancer, and the response was phenomenal. Phone calls and letters poured in, and I received multiple awards, including one from the American Cancer Society for raising awareness and inspiring the largest turnout for mammograms in their history. Women who had survived breast cancer told me that in crying for Lillian they were finally able to cry for themselves. It was an amazing feeling to be able to help women, to show them there were answers and let them know they were not alone. During that time, I painted a scar on my breast to salute the real victims, and whenever I was at the gym or in the tub, it reminded me of what it was like to live with the reality of breast cancer. This was one of those remarkable moments when daytime television really changed people's lives in a way that no straightforward public service announcement ever could.

I was so grateful to Jill Farren-Phelps, who was our producer at that time, for letting me do the story. And that, ultimately, is what I have always felt makes soap opera so very special: its unique ability to pull viewers into the lives of its characters and make them learn and feel something about human frailties and triumphs that they wouldn't experience anywhere else. Soaps are, quite simply, magnified life. And perhaps that's why the people who work together on them become so close to one another at the end of the day. In our roles, we celebrate the holidays together, go to weddings together, go on trips together, rejoice when babies are born or when love trumps all, and deliver eulogies at the funerals of people we've known for years. The life of your character becomes a kind of alternate reality, especially when you've been playing that character for years and years. It doesn't matter that the trees are fake or that the set gets taken down at the end of the day. You have to call on something within yourself to make it real for the audience, and after a while, in many ways, it becomes real for you.

Despite all the years of wonderful memories, there were times when it wasn't as easy for me to love the show. Just as real life goes in cycles, my time on *Guiding Light* had both peaks and the inevitable valleys. In part, this was because I faced the realities of aging on the show before I faced them in real life. Lillian became a grandmother when I was in my forties, and I weathered the changes in her character that accompanied this shift in identity. No one knows more about aging than a soap opera actress who started out as the star, then became the mother of the star, and then became the GRANDMOTHER of the star. If you are a woman in the acting world, your looks are prized; the wisdom and experience that come with age are not.

When I had first arrived on *Somerset* so many years ago, I'd shared a dressing room with a woman named Karla. Karla was one of the older, established actresses on the show, and the room was filled with her things—dried flowers, statuettes from various award shows, and photos of herself when she was young. When I tried to move some of her belongings to make room for mine, she flew into a rage. "How dare you move my things aside and put your things there! What are you trying to do, take over? It's always the way with you young actresses, you have no respect for those of us who have been working on this show for decades. I have been using this room for twenty years, my dear, and you are not to forget that. If you do, you can find someplace else to dress."

> *No one knows more about aging than a soap opera actress who started out as the star, then became the mother of the star, and then became the GRANDMOTHER of the star.*

Fortunately, I was performing so much on the show that I didn't have to worry about being stuck in that little room with Karla. A few weeks later I came into work and she was gone. The room had been emptied out completely. I never found out what happened to her.

But as I got older, I began to understand where Karla was coming from. Every career woman of a certain age knows what it's like to wake up one day and realize that there is a whole new generation of young, pretty up-and-comers at your heels. And it often happens without us realizing it. As I approached my fifties, the younger actresses on the show claimed the spotlight more and more, while Lillian and I began to fade into the background.

Each week when the new scripts arrived at my apartment, it became harder to deny that a shift was taking place. Gone were the juicy plotlines and steamy love interests of my earlier days; now my story lines were all about other characters, not me. All I ever seemed to do was wander the town of Springfield asking various people, "Where's Beth?" It was as though I didn't exist except as a foil for my daughter. "Where's Beth?" "Have you seen Beth?" I must have said that line twenty thousand times.

I wasn't the only one going through "the diminishing" as I called it. One of the best actors on the show, who was a good friend of mine and of similar age, was starting to feel it, too. One day he came into my dressing room and said, "Goddammit! How can you stand it, Tina? Watching them write us out of the show. I've been standing around here all day long just to say two words. Two words! My one line in the scene—'Are they . . .'—isn't even a complete sentence! 'Are they . . .' What kind of line is that?" He paused and then said, "I'm getting out of my contract. I'm out of here. Why do you keep coming back? When's the last time you said anything other than 'Where's Beth?' They're doing the same thing to you, doll face."

And sure enough, he left the show. But his question—why did I keep doing it?—haunted me. I tried not to feel slighted by the change in stature and the paltry lines. I knew that I was extremely lucky to still have a role on a soap opera at my age; I was close to sixty, and in the acting world, sixty is considered really old—especially if you're a woman. But the new reality ate away at me, especially when I saw the younger actresses charging down to the set to do yet another love scene. It was painful to watch them doing what I used to do and realize that I would never have that kind of role again.

It was also around this time that Lillian's white high heels—the sleek, stylish shoes that I'd been wearing to work at Cedars Hospital for years—disappeared as well. The producers decided that the hospital staff should start wearing scrubs because that's what nurses and orderlies now did in the real world. So my pressed, white uniform vanished and the high-heeled shoes went with it. And what did they have me wear on my feet instead?

SNEAKERS. Ugh. I had definitely come down in the world.

I began to look at the younger actresses in a way that I never had before. They appeared on set in a continuous stream, each one prettier than the last. And the more excited they were about what they were doing, the more neglected and ignored I felt. They would sometimes stop by my dressing room to chat, and ask me if they should wear the blue lingerie or the black, and didn't I think the black was sexier, or could I even believe how cute Jim, their partner in the love scene, was, or if their hair was too blond, or if their tan was wearing off, or—my all-time favorite—"Tina, did you ever have to do love scenes when you were younger?" I now understood why Karla had hated me all those years before. It was as though we were from different planets: Planet Young and Lovely, and Planet Old and Boring.

The low point came when we filmed our Christmas show in 2000, the annual episode in which all the characters gathered at the Spaulding mansion for the Christmas party. Everyone was decked out in ball gowns and tuxedos, and the set was lavishly decorated with a soaring, twelve-foot tree that glittered with vintage glass ornaments and tiny white lights. We all looked forward to this episode every year as it felt like a real holiday party for the cast and crew. But that year, when it came time to stage the party scene, I was put at the very back of the room. Everybody else—even the new kids who had only been there for two or three months—was out in front. No one would even see me. And it was devastating. All I could think was, "Doesn't anybody want me?" After we filmed the scene, I went back to my dressing room, closed the door, and cried.

And I wondered, Is this all that is left for me? To fade away into the background and just disappear? I had never felt anything except fabulous about being on the show. But now I wasn't sure. Maybe it was time to quit. I didn't want to stop acting, but maybe I was just too old. They wanted new faces, younger faces.

Still, I showed up for work every day I was called to deliver my one or two lines:

"Here are the results of your MRI!" (Smile.)

"Time to take your temperature!" (Smile.)

"Where's Beth?" (Smile.) "Has anyone seen Beth?"

Where's Tina? Has anyone seen Tina?

After my friend broke his contract and left the show, I couldn't help but wonder if I should do the same. Perhaps it would be better to leave now rather than suffer further diminishment or the humiliation of being written off. But something inside me just couldn't walk away. Despite my moments of wounded pride, I still truly loved acting. I still got a lift from being on set. I loved the hair and makeup people and the other actors on the show. They were my family away from my family. I couldn't imagine giving all that up. And the perks—the perks were marvelous: upgrades on planes; hotels that refused to let you pay; people you could meet and talk to that you otherwise would never know;

Emmy ceremonies; recognition at restaurants; amazing clothes; the wonderful income; the pride of my husband and son; and on and on.

And besides, let's face it—there aren't that many roles for aging women out there. This was certainly one of the prime reasons that I stayed on as Lillian. Once I had passed the age of forty-five, I knew that there would be fewer and fewer other roles that I could potentially play. Lillian wasn't a spicy, focal character like Reva or Phillip Spaulding—but she was still a solid role on a great show, so I was practical about it. If I gave up my role on *Guiding Light*, there was no guaranteeing what was next.

I gave it some thought and realized that I really wanted to keep working. In fact, I NEEDED to keep working. Not so much for the money as for the purpose it gave me. Being a part of the show made me feel relevant. It gave me someplace to go in the mornings and kept me engaged with the world. Things would have to change, because I knew I couldn't go on standing at the back of the Christmas party, or hiding out in my dressing room eating M&M'S and feeling sorry for myself. I would have to find a way to convince the writers and producers that Lillian did have life in her yet. But in the meantime, I wasn't going anywhere.

And so I came to what is perhaps the most important lesson in managing our careers as we get older: Sometimes staying in the game is as simple as not leaving the room.

When I had been on *Guiding Light* for about ten years, I experienced firsthand the power of the show's writers. For some strange reason, Lillian had been promoted to chairman of Cedars Hospital—with absolutely no qualifications, let me add. Overnight, I suddenly had authority over the entire hospital and staff.

I was holding meetings telling the board how to get funding and discussing whether we should build new wings; I was hiring and firing, and best of all, I was now wearing fabulous designer clothes like everyone else. I was so, so, so happy!

But then our very talented head writer and her husband separated, and a real-life drama ensued. The husband, who was an actor on the show, happened to be a very, very good friend of mine, and what do you know, the minute he and his wife separated, Lillian got demoted. Suddenly I was saying lines like, "You know, I really want to go back to nursing," or "I miss being with patients," and *boom*, all in one day I was back to the little white uniform and bringing people pills. Good-bye pretty clothes, good-bye powerful woman telling the board what to do. I really did love being a nurse, so it wasn't terrible, but it was such an insight into the politics of the show. It was a great way for her to punish me for being on her husband's side.

When I began to take stock of my future on *Guiding Light*, I knew that the writers had the power to decide my fate, and that above all, I had to avoid being sent to Dr. Death. After all, once the writers decide that it's time to get rid of your character, there's very little you can do about it. So I would have to reinvent myself in a way that not only made sense for the show, but also allowed me to reclaim some of the presence I had lost.

Frankly, as much as I loved Lillian, there was no denying that she was a perfect candidate for a makeover. While she'd seen her fair share of drama throughout the years, the essence of her character hadn't changed all that much from those first early days as Bradley's wife. She was generally passive, letting things happen to her rather than standing up for herself. She was timid about basic things like flying on planes, and she fretted about Beth constantly but never took a hard line on her behavior. Especially in recent years, she had become this kind of plodding, good, and rather dull woman who would sit at home with her cat and watch *Gone with the Wind*. The writers would actually show her at home alone doing these things, and I'd just want to shake her and say, "Oh, Lillian, get some life!"

So I began—in the nicest way possible—to make suggestions to the writers about story lines for Lillian. While some actresses would have screamed and stomped their feet until they got their way, I recognized that you can't get away with that approach unless you are incredibly valuable—and at sixty, very few of us are perceived that way. And by the way, I cannot abide screaming and yelling.

I wasn't going to win by going to the writers and producers and telling them that I was only sixty and needed more to do—to them sixty was really, really old. When I was younger, I'd seen older actresses desperately trying to defend their turf and it didn't work. They would start demanding inappropriate story lines and dressing young, never realizing that it only made them look like more of a has-been. This happens in any industry or workplace. You can't be a diva and expect to remain the center of attention, the queen holding court, when it's time to let go. There comes a time when younger people are supposed to supplant us in our profession, and we really have no choice but to be graceful about it and support them as they pick up where we left off. I really got behind this idea and never complained about being left out. Instead I joined the parade and applauded them.

And all of a sudden, things started happening for Lillian. On a soap, the writers are always trying to bring the various families together and get them tangled up in each other's lives, so I suggested to the head writer, my friend Jill Hurst, that Lillian, who was living with the Spauldings at the time, go on a date with Buzz

Cooper. She loved the idea and before I knew it, Lillian was part of a romantic story line for the first time in years! Lillian and Buzz—or "Lillibuzz" as the fans called us—became one of the sweetest and most likable couples on the show. Justin Deas and I had a terrific time with that story. And needless to say, the older female viewers were thrilled to see someone who looked like them having a full-fledged romance (complete with Viagra and an illicit romp in the woods—Lillian and Buzz were certainly forever frisky).

> *We need to be generous with the women following in our footsteps in the hope that they will be generous with us.*

In addition, Lillian was connected to practically the entire town of Springfield in some way, either through Beth's marriages or her work at the hospital, and this worked to my advantage because she was very helpful in facilitating other plotlines. She could be the confidante or the sounding board or the go-between or the person who happened to see so-and-so sneaking out of the house with his brother's wife and had to decide what to do with such scandalous information, and it made perfect sense for her be involved in all these stories. Plus, because I had never been a prima donna or treated any of the other actors badly, everyone was happy to work with me.

I think that every woman, no matter what her profession, gets to a point as she gets older when she needs to make peace with her changing reality, and say to herself, "Okay, I've had my day in the sun. I've had my day when I was the bright, young talent, and I had this great job and it was fabulous. And now I don't have these things anymore. But I'm glad these other women are having them." We cannot allow ourselves to become bitter like Karla. We need to be generous with the women following in our footsteps in the hope that they will be generous with us.

So I did two things. First, if I saw someone new on the show—say, a gorgeous, young blonde they'd recently hired—I would get to know her. I'd make her my friend, because then I wouldn't feel resentful. I'd actually been doing this since the fourth grade when an adorable new girl named Karen Leckie arrived in school and was instantly the most popular girl in class. I'd approached her and we found out we had the same birthday and soon enough we were best friends. Now, decades later, it was the same with the younger actresses on the show; usually I ended up really liking them, and found that interacting with them gave me a boost.

I also tried to think of myself as a mentor, someone who could offer advice and guidance to these young actors about navigating a career in soaps. After all, I'd been around long enough that I'd learned a few things about the business, not to mention the politics of *Guiding Light* itself. I'd seen a lot of actors come and go, and yet, I was still here. I'd also done movies, raised a family, had a thirty-five-year marriage . . . all of which had taught me plenty about balancing work on the show with a life outside. Beth Chamberlin, who played my soap opera daughter Beth, and I had had this kind of relationship for a long time. We'd always stood up for each other and gone to bat for each other even though we were a generation apart. Over the years I'd offered her advice on everything from how to play a scene to having children, and she had offered me advice on how to play a scene (probably the same scene) and exercise and nutrition. She is like a daughter to me. Now I saw that I could have a similar kind of relationship with lots of the other young actors, and Rob Bogue (A. C. Mallet),

Bonnie Dennison (Daisy Lemay), Mandy Bruno (Marina Cooper Camaletti), Karla Mosley (Christina Moore Boudreau), Lawrence Saint-Victor (Remy Boudreau), Caitlin Van Zandt (Ashlee Wolfe), Orlagh Cassidy (Doris Wolfe), Zack Conroy (my grandson, James Spaulding), and Marcy Rylan (my granddaughter, Lizzie Spaulding) all came into the sphere of people I loved spending time with, even though they were a generation or two below me.

And then something interesting started to happen. When I changed the way I approached the show, Lillian began to change, too. The writers began incorporating a little more "Tina" into the scripts and suddenly Lillian was standing up for herself in a way she never had before. This was also around the time that we began shooting with handheld cameras, which allowed a lot more room for improvisation, so I could have fun with the lines in a way that made Lillian stronger. I would stand up to Alan Spaulding, who had murdered dozens of people, or even finally really berate Beth: "Beth, you're sleeping with every man imaginable. Stop it! Get over yourself!" Sometimes what I said wasn't the line at all, but it was always the truth. And people loved it. Lillian became the voice of the audience in those last years, saying whatever it was THEY wanted to say. I would call people out on their bad behavior in a way that no one else did, and this led to some really wonderful scenes. And I began working more and more.

It might sound silly, but I truly believe that karma does affect your working life in later years. If you're not making things better for the people around you, there's very little reason for those who are in charge to keep you on. When I started giving back to the show, all that positive energy seemed to come back to me and Lillian. And it wasn't just the story line with Buzz or the clever improvisations that brought us back into the center of the action. One day we were all standing around during rehearsal and one of the writers said, "You know, we all love Lillian. She's very nurturing, she's very good. She's this warm, constant presence that we all really appreciate having on the show." At the end of the day, people really liked her. She was comfortable, a familiar face that could be counted on to do the right thing, to offer a kind word or a helping hand. And she was always ready to romp in the woods with Buzz.

Hmmm. Maybe Lillian and I weren't so different after all.

I met a very handsome man recently who told me that he "failed retirement." Of course he was so handsome that I might have agreed with anything he was saying, but I think a lot of us feel this way. There is a store in Manhattan on the Upper East Side with a sign in the window that says, "What you make is important." It's a quote by the designer George Nelson, and during my dark times on *Guiding Light*, I would stop and stare at those words as though they'd been put there just for me. I had already begun writing this book, and I realized that I was writing it to help every woman, including myself, get through this time of diminishment—and that what I was making WAS IMPORTANT. I've always known that without work, without making something, I would be adrift like a tiny rowboat in a massive sea. This was, of course, why I fought so hard to maintain my role on the show—I loved making Lillian come alive for the fans and for myself.

So you can imagine how devastating it was to learn that CBS had decided to cancel *Guiding Light*, the show that had been the emotional history of our country for seventy-two years. We found out on April Fool's Day 2009, and we were all stunned. It was crushing. All of us—the directors and producers, the cast and the crew, including all the lighting, sound, hair, and makeup people—

were in tears. We just couldn't believe it. I had been on the show for nearly three decades. It was my routine and my life and my calling card and my joy, and I knew that I would be incredibly lonely without it—AND without Lillian. I had lived side by side with this woman for so long and couldn't imagine that she was just going to disappear into the vapors. When she vanished, would I disappear, too?

I couldn't let that happen. Not just for me, but for all the fans who loved and knew her and watched her for so many years. Lillian has become a part of me, and as long as I am performing, she is there with me. It was the fans that allowed me to keep playing Lillian; if they hadn't been watching and responding to her story lines she would have made the trip to Dr. Death long ago. Now, as I change my shoes, I keep all of those fans with me, and every time I walk onstage or on set to perform, it is a chance for me to thank them for the wonderful years they gave to me.

I knew that I couldn't let this be the end of my life as an actress. And I knew I definitely didn't want to retire. Steve and I knew CEOs and captains of industry who had practically fallen apart after they retired; without their jobs and their companies they were left to putter around the house and became obsessed with things like lining up the forks in the dishwasher perfectly and in general drove both themselves and their wives crazy. I had bounced back once before during my dark years on the show and I knew that I could do it again. I realized, with incredible sadness, that my time on soaps was probably over. But there were other things I could potentially do: films, theater, writing. I recalled how Matisse had been forced to reinvent himself as he aged, trading his paints for brightly colored collages when his arthritic hands could no longer hold a paintbrush. And I remembered Aga's wisdom: You just have to change your shoes. Now that Lillian's nursing sneakers would be going the way of her white high heels, I would have to find new shoes to wear in my professional life.

So I began thinking more about the book I'd been working on that contained many memories of my years on *Guiding Light*, and other soaps as well as my early career. At that point, it was a shell of a book, but it was also full of stories and lessons about aging, and I began to wonder if it might work as a play. I mean, I was an actress and now I had some free time (lots of free time), so I talked to a brilliant young teacher I knew, Joe Plummer, who was teaching a class I was taking on Shakespeare and had a Shakespeare company called Poor Tom Productions. After seeing one of his productions, I gave him a first draft of this book and asked if he thought it might work for the theater.

We began working on a rough script together. We met at my apartment at seven every night and he would have dinner with Steve and me in the kitchen, and then Joe and I would retire to the dining room and work, work, work. We would argue and laugh and write and argue some more, and the whole process began to take on a life of its own. This was exciting for me, as I hadn't done any theater since my very early acting days in New York. We were perfectly mismatched as Joe was young and I wasn't, he was steeped in theater and I wasn't, he was about Shakespeare and I was about soap opera, but somehow the differences in us worked and we gave birth to the play *Changing Shoes*.

And it was terrifying, too—the prospect that this show might actually come together and I'd have to go onstage every night LIVE in front of hundreds of people. But it gave me something to hold on to during those heartbreaking days when we were filming the last episodes of the show. It enabled me to see beyond Lillian to something that, while it could NEVER replace my role on *Guiding Light*, could be fulfilling in other ways. There JUST

MIGHT BE life after Lillian Raines. I had to put on new shoes, and get out there and find it.

My friend Jean had faced a similar challenge after losing her husband, a famous writer. For years, she had been at home raising their daughter and helping her husband with his books, which was no small task. He was constantly speaking and traveling, and she was involved with many nonprofit organizations, and it took an enormous amount of time to manage it all. But they were a great team: Jean had been a reporter herself years before, so they were a perfectly matched pair of intellectuals and she was an ideal sounding board for much of her husband's work.

After his sudden death, Jean knew it was time to figure out what the next step was for her; she knew she didn't just want to be a keeper of the flame. "It's really about finding purpose in your life," she told me. "If you don't have a purpose, there's an emptiness. Working gives you a sense of forward motion." So she used her connections in the nonprofit world to find a job with the National Park Service. "I'm paid less per hour than I was making thirty years ago at *The New York Times*," she says with a laugh. "But I have a lot of freedom with the hours, the office is in a great location, and I enjoy it. The truth is that when you're sixty years old, nobody's going to give you a hundred-thousand-dollar-a-year job. Even if you had that job twenty years ago, it's not going to be there for you. So, you need to find something else. You either create it yourself, or maybe, like me, you figure out what you're good at and start volunteering and it turns into something more."

My friend Laura, an event planner, agrees: "It's true that it doesn't come as easily as it used to. When you're younger, opportunities find you. Now you need to be a lot more proactive. But what you get from working changes, too, and in a good way. I've always enjoyed my job, but ten years ago, the work I did was for my children—so that they could have things or go to camp or get a good education. Now my work is for me, to keep me busy. My clients keep me tuned in to new ideas and trends, and I get to travel and meet all sorts of different people. Working definitely keeps me from feeling old."

Even my soap opera daughter, Beth, professed when the show was winding down that closing one chapter of our professional lives doesn't have to mean the end of who we are—or that we can't go on to something else that is just as rewarding. Change often leads us somewhere interesting, whether we've looked for it or not. "It's a strange feeling," she confessed to me when we were taping

> *Change often leads us somewhere interesting, whether we've looked for it or not.*

the last few episodes of *Guiding Light*. "I grew up on this show in so many ways, I can't imagine not coming to the set every day. But at the same time, I feel like I'm starting a new cycle in my life. And that's a good thing. It feels like it's time for something new."

The day that we taped the very last episode of *Guiding Light* was a warm, late-summer day in Peapack, New Jersey. It had already been an emotional week—we all kept tearing up, especially when we realized that we were about to shoot our final scene with a certain character, or that story lines we had been a part of for years had finally been resolved. When I taped my last scene with Beth, we were both so sad we could hardly look at each other. But there were a lot of amazing moments and highs as well. Lillian married Buzz in a double wedding with one of the show's favorite and equally "mature" couples, Billy (played by the great Jordan Clarke) and Vanessa (played by my dear friend Maeve Kincaid). I got to wear a gorgeous wedding dress with white high-heeled sandals and walk down the aisle with flowers in my hair. And Josh and Reva met at the lighthouse and declared their undying love, and decided to set off on an adventure together with Reva's son. Beth and Phillip married (again), as did Rick and Mindy. Alan died peacefully after saving Phillip's life. My granddaughter, Lizzie, and her husband were going to have a baby. Alex went off into the sunset with Fletcher. And on and on the happy endings went.

But the best part of all was the line that Buzz said to me during our wedding vows. It summed up the entire show for me, and while I'll never know exactly why the writers gave it to him, I couldn't help but think it had something to do with the fact that I'd stayed loyal to the show for all those years. He said, "Lillian, you are the light that guides me."

I knew then that I had been right to stay, that my work on the show had really mattered to many people other than just me. Instead of stepping aside or giving up, I was now going out in a blaze of glory. Whatever rough spots I'd weathered as Lillian Raines, being there to hear that line made it all worth it.

The Key to Your Working Life: Staying Flexible

When I was working with Beverlee McKinsey, she loved to tell stories about her years on *Guiding Light*. One of her most famous anecdotes took place back in the days when soaps were live—live, not taped, so there were no second chances. In this particular scene, Beverlee and another actor were having a conversation while standing over the bed of a guy who was supposedly paralyzed. But this was also in the days when the actors smoked, and as they stood there, a lit ash fell off one of their cigarettes onto the chest of the paralyzed guy. He hollered and jumped up and then stood there. Everybody was quiet. And then Beverlee said, "It's a miracle!"

They had to change the story line totally after that. And it demonstrates what I believe is the most important thing we need to do if we want to stay in the game professionally as we get older: Be flexible and roll with the punches. You're not going to be able to continue being successful at your job by doing it the same way you've always done it. And it's difficult to face the reality that things that worked for you in the past aren't quite cutting it anymore. But the times have changed and so have you. So you'll need to evolve in order to keep yourself relevant.

Stay on top of the trends within your industry and try to incorporate them as best you can. For me, flexibility has meant learning to use an iPod, the iPhone, the Amazon

Kindle, Twitter, and a host of other "techy" things that I could just as easily have ignored. I've also made an effort to keep honing my craft: I take a course in Shakespeare once a week in the evenings and have taught acting seminars for young people. My one-woman show has also been a tremendous growth experience—I never thought I could be on-stage for more than an hour all by myself, but now I've done it and been a success, and I plan on doing the show *Changing Shoes* for years to come.

If you find that you are forced to retire or make a change, remember that we are all more than our trademarks. Today, many people I know are enjoying so-called Encore Careers that are quite different from what they used to do. Our life's work does define a part of who we are, but we are so much more and now is the time to find that hidden person. Maybe you want to teach or learn to ice-skate or take up French cooking or be a volunteer for the Red Cross. This phase of life is a great time to discover the OTHER you. Most important, we need to tune out the voice that says, "I could have been . . ." or "I should have been . . ." These thoughts will immobilize you and prevent you from moving forward. Instead of saying, "I could have been," just get up—now—and go be it.

CHAPTER FIVE

Being Out in Front

Of all the roles I've had throughout my life, being a mother is the one I love the most. While I got to play Beth's mother every day on *Guiding Light*, at home I was the real-life mother of my son, Renny. Nothing quite prepared me for the transforming experience of becoming a parent, and from the moment Renny was born, I was totally enthralled. Of course being a mother is very different from playing a mother on a soap opera. It didn't take long for me to realize just how different it was. As Beth's mother on the soap opera I could spend hours running through the woods searching for her after she went missing (yet again), which you would think would be exhausting, yet somehow never was. I always emerged from those woods looking freshly coiffed and made-up. In reality as Renny's mother I looked haggard and worn down after just a few sleepless nights. As Beth's mother the emotional drain was intense—after all she had been raped, murdered, and abused—but none of it compared with the emotional drain I experienced when Renny had the slightest sniffle.

I was thirty-six when I finally had Renny, but getting there was a soap opera all its own. It seemed, at some point in my late twenties, that all of my friends became pregnant overnight, and as I walked across town to the CBS Studios, children just seemed to be everywhere. Renny was a longed-for but unexpected gift, as for years, I'd thought that I would probably never have children. While I was able to get pregnant easily, unfortunately I wasn't able to stay pregnant. By the time he arrived, I'd had eight miscarriages. But Steve and I desperately wanted a baby, so I was willing to risk the heartache of another failed attempt. After my seventh miscarriage I had started to give up and after the eighth I resigned myself to the fact that I was never going to have a child. And then, lo and behold, my ninth pregnancy took. I had amniocentesis, so we knew it was a boy, and somehow that made me feel much less fragile—I started walking differently and being more active, because I knew that this child was going to be a fighter. I didn't tell anyone about the pregnancy—I was afraid that I might jinx it. But after the fourth month passed without incident I couldn't keep it a secret any longer. Our friends were thrilled for us and I had showers upon showers and parties and gifts, and got the nursery ready—I had the walls done in blue with white clouds painted on the ceiling. I had gone baby crazy! And five months later, at six thirty A.M. on July 19, in the middle of a 104-degree Manhattan heat wave with no air-conditioning in the hospital, our son, Renny, was born.

We named him Forbes Reynolds McPherson. Steve always says it sounds like a law firm; I thought it sounded like a soap opera character. The truth is, he was named after both our fathers: My father was Forbes and Steve's father was Reynolds. At first it seemed like a big name for a tiny baby, but from the start, Renny was wise. He seemed to wear an expression of wisdom beyond his years. He almost never cried, just gazed up at me with these big green eyes framed by red-gold hair. Overnight our apartment was filled with diapers and formula and cribs and car seats and strollers, and I couldn't believe how wonderful and startling it was to suddenly have another full person there. But the biggest change of all, as any parent will tell you, was realizing how much one can love another person. Like every other first-time parent I thought no other child had ever crawled or cooed or smiled in the history of the world before Renny. Nothing in my history of playing mothers on television had prepared me for being a mother in real life.

I remember thinking that it was all worth it—the wait and sadness of losing babies to get this one, this child that was mine. I wanted him to be near me all the time. I took him to restaurants and museums and theaters and friends' houses, and he just went along and smiled. And because of my acting, he grew up with an amazing group of honorary relatives. Betty Buckley, who first sang "Memory" in *Cats* on Broadway, would come by and sing him lullabies, and my friend Cathy, who was also a Broadway singer, would come over to help with meals or the bath and sing to him the entire time.

Every stage brought something new, and when Renny started talking, I was even more enchanted. I couldn't get enough of his baby talk, that charming mix of words and non-words that toddlers babble all day long. He once told me I looked like "Cindalella" because of my blond hair. And once when he was about three, I had to go to California for work and asked his nursery school teacher if I should take him with me. She said, "Oh, he'll want to stay in school. He really loves it," but when I asked Renny what he wanted to do, he said, "I will go with Mommy to Balbornia." Balbornia! Who could resist?

Even as a young child, Renny was incredibly concentrated about everything he did in life. Whatever he did, he was very involved and focused, and as his parents, Steve and I became involved, too. Like many little boys, Renny was obsessed with cars, and he had dozens of toy cars and trucks lined up along the shelves in his room. Friends who came to visit wouldn't dare arrive without a toy car or truck in hand, and he'd go right up to them and say, "More car? Two car? Big car?" He used to walk around with them in his hands, never wanting to set them down, even for a moment. He could tell you who had given him which car and he had managed to get what seemed like hundreds.

He also loved to look at license plates, and that became our family game, to see if we could find one from every state. Manhattan draws cars from all over the country, and after a while Renny was able to recognize all the different plates. He'd spot them on the street and shout, "Texas!" or "Maine!" We kept a list in his room of the ones we'd seen, and over time, we found license plates from every single state . . . except Kansas.

One night, Steve came home late from the office. It was past ten o'clock and Renny was already in bed, but Steve came bursting in the door, and said, "Get him up! There's a Kansas out in front!" So we got Renny up and bundled him into his coat and took him outside so he could see Kansas. When he saw it his eyes lit up. Something so simple made all three of us so happy.

We always spent our summers in a tiny beach community on a small island—the kind of place where friendships are formed that last for generations, and children grow up and marry and then come back with their children. We were renters, so we had a number of different houses over the years. Family was an integral

part of life there and it was easy to find ways to spend time together. We would ride bikes or go to the beach, and gather with
our neighbors every Fourth of July to watch the fireworks over
the harbor. Renny and I would play tennis matches against other
parents and their children and we always lost and it was always my
fault. "Mom," Renny would ask, disappointed, "why did you keep
hitting the ball into the net?" and I would laugh and shrug my
shoulders.

It was those special summers that gave me one of my favorite
pairs of shoes—a pair of lime green espadrilles that I wore everywhere from the golf club to the beach, and for me came to signify
everything delicious about those summers: cookouts on the beach;
the smell of salt air and suntan lotion; eating lobsters; and building sand castles. Once when I was wearing them, Renny and I
went to the local store and bought some tiny pies—pumpkin,
chocolate cream, and lemon meringue—and took them down to
a deserted part of the beach and had a real, honest-to-goodness
pie fight. We ran up and down the dunes, chasing each other,
smearing the whipped cream all over our faces, licking our fingers
and laughing until our sides hurt. Those espadrilles took a beating and I could never quite get the sand out of them, even after
we'd returned to the city. But I wore them for years, and I loved to
see their vibrant color in my closet during the winter when the
beach seemed very far away.

Steve's two children, Genie and Sandy, were often a part of
our family outings, and by this point, we had all blended very
well. Renny looked up to them and admired them tremendously,
as they were more than fifteen years older. Still, like any family of
five, we had to work at balancing everyone's needs. Steve's children
understandably wanted his time, and Renny wanted both our
time, and Steve wanted MY time since like most husbands, he

was a little bit jealous of how much of my love and attention went to Renny. But we all tried hard to make room for one another, especially for Steve's sake, as he was the one most often caught in the middle.

One year, on his fiftieth birthday, Steve decided that it would be a grand idea for us all to take a vacation together. Now I have always advocated that one should do whatever one wishes on one's fiftieth birthday. A friend of ours took a plane around the world so he could celebrate his birthday over and over again in every time zone, which was rather original but also meant that he spent all that time flying on a plane, which wouldn't have been my choice. But Steve came up with what he thought was the perfect fiftieth celebration for him: He would take all of us, including Renny who was six, on a backpacking trip on horseback in the Sawtooth Mountains of Montana.

He came to tell me this wreathed in smiles—he'd worked the whole thing out in secret with a guide in Bozeman, Montana, because he wanted it to be a surprise. Oh, it was! We would be going up into the mountains on HORSES and camping in TENTS for a whole week with a six-year-old! But it was his birthday, and he'd arranged it down to the last detail, so a few days later, we all gathered at the airport: Me, Steve, Renny, and Genie and Sandy, who were eighteen and twenty-two at the time.

In his younger days, Steve had been a ranger in Yellowstone National Park, so he was very much in love with the grandeur of the outdoors. He had bought us all cowboy hats and boots and jeans and work shirts, but in our clean, brand-new outfits, we still looked like total city slickers. Steve was also very much in love with horses, and rode beautifully. The rest of us trembled as we met our horses for the week. Mine, of course, immediately noticed I was trembling. She was a gold and white horse named

Daisy, an imposing mare, and she seemed to know that I was terrified of her. I was sure she was giving me a mocking smile every time she bared her teeth.

After several tries, I finally hoisted myself up onto the saddle, and Daisy immediately began trying to force me right back off again. She started walking and proceeded to push me into some bushes and trees. The idea that I would be spending a week with this holy terror seemed a flat-out impossibility. I looked around for the others, who all seemed far more assured—even Renny, on his huge horse, appeared in control.

Finally, we set out and Daisy made sure that we were last in line, and as we all went around a corner to start up the mountain, she turned and began heading in a different direction. When I tried to pull on the reins to get her to join the others, she turned her head and BIT MY FOOT. She then began heading back down toward the camp. I cajoled and hummed and patted and cried, and when our guide finally came back to see where we were, as we had gotten lost barely three minutes into the trip, Daisy immediately turned around and trotted behind him obediently as though she was an angel and I was the one who'd chosen a diversionary route.

We fished for our dinners and sang songs, and somehow we made it up and down the mountain and bonded over the hardships of the trip (except for me and Daisy—every day she would pretend to slip going down steep slopes, or pretend not to notice that I was on her and rear up, or pretend to like me as I gave her an apple and then nip at my fingers when she took it from me. But she was the only one who acted up—the rest of the family behaved.).

We were thrilled ten years later when Steve turned sixty and announced that he wanted to go to Italy. It's much easier to be one big, happy extended family (by this time we'd acquired a son-in-law and several grandchildren) when everyone has access to a shower and a comfortable bed. I was especially relieved knowing there was no chance of running into Daisy on the hills of Tuscany.

But as vivid as all these memories still seem, Renny didn't stay a little boy for long. Despite the fact that he was my earth and stars, and I was the sun and moon to him, he grew up to be his own person. As any parent will tell you, this happens much more rapidly than you ever expected. Before I knew it, he had breezed through elementary school and middle school, and was now thriving in high school and well on his way to college. No longer was I the sun and the moon, but I was still Mom and I was needed in other ways. I was the cook/chauffeur/facilitator/advisor, and I happily did all these things—kept the refrigerator stocked with his favorite foods, delivered him to friends' houses, and was there and available and NONJUDGMENTAL if and when he ever needed advice. If he wanted to go skiing with his pals, I would make the arrangements, find another mom to come along, and be there to provide meals and hot chocolate. If he needed a cool costume for a Halloween party, I would ask Shawn and Alyson, the costume designers on *Guiding Light,* what they had that I could work with. Of course the real trick was to do all these things without seeming to be doing anything at all. Teenagers value their independence, and they ARE independent in so many ways, but they still need the assistance and protective covering that only a parent can provide.

Once Renny got to college, his life was more and more his own, and he began doing most of these things for himself. We would go up to Cambridge every weekend to see him row for the Harvard freshman heavyweight crew, and it always struck me how strong and self-sufficient he was. When he was home on vacation, he still liked to chat, but it was always between comings and goings. Most mothers will tell you that they hang around the house when their kids are home from school in hopes of snatching a brief conversation between parties. And let me tell you, Renny coming home was always the highlight of my life, even if I was filming a movie with Al Pacino. But now our relationship was more of a give-and-take; sometimes I asked HIM for advice, instead of just vice versa. Still, the ties that held him to us remained. During his freshman year, Renny wrote a story for a creative writing class and the professor told him, "This dialogue is very realistic!" Renny replied, "That's because my mom is on a soap opera, and I ran dialogue with her for fifteen years." And one time on my birthday, he made me a list of all the reasons—some hilarious and some sweet—that I had been a great mother, including, "You took me on the Small World ride eighty-two times in a row," "Your slippers make a funny noise," and "You come to me whenever I ask you to." Our history as parents, whatever it is, always leaves a mark. But inevitably we were becoming known more and more as "Renny's parents" and he was becoming less and less "Tina and Steve's son."

In the soap opera world, children come and go and disappear and reappear and everyone takes it in stride. When I was on *Guiding Light* Beth had another daughter besides Lizzie who we never even saw—she was born and then we totally forgot her and she didn't exist. I even had a line one time when I said to Beth, "You only have one daughter and she's about to get married." And I was just thinking, "No, no, no, she had two daughters!" but the writers didn't remember. (She also had a son named James who we never saw, but was always "upstairs in the computer room" until he emerged at around age eighteen. And yet he was supposedly happy and well-adjusted whereas Lizzie, who we saw all the time and was attached to Beth's hip, had all the problems and claimed that Beth was never there for her. Talk about the mysteries of parenting.) But in real life the natural distancing of Renny from Steve and me was much more nuanced.

I sometimes think that Renny, being the wise, old soul that he was, knew early on that childhood doesn't last forever. When he was little, like so many children, he used to come and crawl into bed with Steve and me if he'd had a bad dream or simply couldn't sleep. And on the nights before he went off to summer camp, he'd come into our room and lie down at the foot of the bed and stay there, curled up under a blanket, until morning. One night when he was about six years old, he came padding down the hall to our room and climbed in between us, and Steve said, "Come on, Ren, go back to your own bed." But he stayed right where he was and pulled up the covers and said, "You know, Dad, someday you're going to miss having me here. You and Mom are going to miss me when I'm grown-up." And he was so right.

During his sophomore year, Renny told us that one of his friends and fellow rowers had gone to Marine Officers Candidate School in Quantico, Virginia, the summer before and thought it was a great experience. Marine training seemed about as big of a physical challenge as you could possibly get, and Renny thought he might like to give it a try. He talked to some other Marines and decided to do the program that summer and see how he liked it. Naturally the experience is designed to test young men and see if they have what it takes to join the military. But it didn't really occur to me that this was a possibility. Renny had always talked about going into journalism when he finished school, and I just assumed that this would be his path after he graduated.

But he ended up loving his time at Quantico, and that fall, after he was back at Harvard, September 11th took place—so when the OCS recruiter called him up to see if he was coming back the following summer, there was no question. Still, I didn't think he would actually join full-time. I was proud of him for wanting to be involved with the Marines at such an important moment in American history, but somehow I felt certain that come graduation, he'd choose to find a job in New York City, close to home.

Then one day in April of Renny's senior year, I was standing in the kitchen when the phone rang. It was Renny and he sounded serious. He told me that he had committed to join the Marines. COMMITTED, as in past tense. I was completely stunned. How could we be having a conversation about "committed" when we'd never had the conversation "thinking about committing"? I couldn't believe it. Yes, it was noble and honorable, but what would I do if something happened to him? He was my only child.

"Sweetheart," I said, "can we at least talk about this? Why do you have to go in? Wouldn't you rather go to the Iowa Writers' Workshop like you always talked about?"

He said, "Mom, what do you think I've been doing the past two years?"

He was right, of course. There had clearly been denial on my part—after all, most people don't go to Marine OCS for two summers just for fun. But pretending that he wasn't going to actually join the military had been my safety valve, taking the pressure off so I didn't worry. It had allowed me to get through these past two years without constantly thinking about the what-ifs.

But then two alternate scenarios flashed through my mind. That first summer when he'd gone to Quantico, I'd encouraged him to take a position with a friend at the World Trade Center, which had, of course, subsequently been attacked on September 11th. I had also met a man at a party recently who told me that his mother had kept him from going into the Marines, so he had gone to work for an investment firm and been sent to their offices in the Middle East. While there, he was taken hostage and he'd told me, "Here I was, in real danger, with no gun or anything else. If I'd been in the Marines, I would at least have been able to defend myself."

I felt like the universe was sending me a message, and decided right then and there that even if I desperately didn't want him to go in—and I mean, I really, REALLY didn't want him to go in— I would shut up and be supportive and let him lead his own life. After we'd hung up, I just wandered around the apartment trying to grasp what was going to happen. But after that first phone call, I never said another word to try to dissuade him. He had made his decision. It was something he had thought about for several years and obviously really wanted. Steve was thrilled about it and proud of him for joining, and I decided (and this is the important word—*decided*) to hold in all my doubts and fears and be proud of him for serving our country.

He was commissioned at Harvard as a Second Lieutenant the day before graduation. All his friends and family were there, and a Marine Corps General came up from Camp Lejeune, North Carolina, to conduct the ceremony. On that day, Renny's hair was cut short and he was in his glorious dress blues, and there were flags, swords, and fanfare, and it was very emotional for us all. When I pinned his bars on him, I pricked my finger, which bled, and I remember thinking that that was how my heart was feeling—but I wasn't going to show anyone. This was his life, and his challenge, and my challenge was to back him up.

He had another year of training in Virginia, and we went down to see him when they had a Parents' Visit, and oh, those boys were so amazing and such a tribute to what I think all young men should be. Their parents were remarkable, too, and I was profoundly humbled by all that they were doing, and so proud that Renny was a part of it. While I was there, I was reminded that the motto of the U.S. Marines is SEMPER FI, "ALWAYS FAITHFUL."

It struck me then, and still strikes me now, that those words perfectly capture the relationship between mother and son.

There is perhaps nothing more rewarding for a parent than watching your child grow up and spread his wings—and for many, nothing more quietly heartbreaking at the same time. As we get older, our children begin to take center stage with their graduations and marriages and their own children, and we retreat into the background to become the watchers. When they were younger, we related through the rules they had to live by, and the experiences we shared, and the advice they did and didn't want to hear. Now they have spouses and friends to give them advice, and their own children to love and play with. But we still want to be in the mix. So how do we adjust to this change, the empty nest? And more important, how do we remain a vital part of our children's lives?

These days, whenever Renny comes to visit, I can't wait to do anything that makes me feel like I'm still needed. I'll do his laundry or rush out on wings to buy him socks or make a dinner reservation for him and his girlfriend or whatever else he happens to need. And personally, I love doing all this. If he called me up tomorrow and said, "Mom, could you go to Africa and find a lion for me?" I'd do it in a heartbeat. He is an adult, and he totally takes care of himself and that is the way it is supposed to be. But

> *There is perhaps nothing more rewarding for a parent than watching your child grow up and spread his wings—and for many, nothing more quietly heartbreaking at the same time.*

it feels so good when he needs my help or asks for advice or comes by for a good talk or to watch a football game. If I can have lunch with him while he is in New York City, I'll cancel the Pope. The truth is that when we get to this stage, we still want our children to call us and come visit—and visit A LOT. I once asked Steve if he had any thoughts on how to get Renny to call us more often, and he said, "Be sick a lot." Obviously, he was kidding, but that does make the phone ring.

My friend Lydia is the mother of four boys, and for years, her sons were the center of her world. She was divorced from their father when they were quite young, so she had devoted herself to providing a good life for them. She was fortunate enough to have a successful catering business and a wonderful nanny who loved all four boys like her own sons. For years, their house was full of energy and activity and her days were spent shepherding one to sports practice and another to his piano lesson and the third to his SAT tutor and so on, all while running her business in between. Lydia and the nanny had a huge eraser board on the kitchen wall with the boys' schedules for the week so they could keep track of who was doing what and when. The entire rhythm of their day was determined by the boys and their needs and meals and whereabouts, all the way up until two in the morning.

But eventually, her sons went off to college and then settled on their own and Lydia was left with a big, empty house. "I come from a big Italian family," Lydia told me. "I can't stand the quiet. I love the noise, I love the kids, I love the whirlwind and bustle. For years, our house was always the hangout. One of the boys would come home from school and bring fifteen friends, and I didn't care, I loved having them around. Now I don't see them nearly as much. Two of them are married and things are different.

"When my youngest son first went off to college," she continued, "I must have locked myself out of the house twenty times. For years, I had never needed a key because there was always someone there—either the nanny or one of the boys. So I'd fallen out of the habit of carrying one. That was a hard realization," she recalled. "That there was no one home anymore. I needed to bring my keys with me."

Three of Lydia's sons found good jobs in New York, but the youngest moved to Seattle and the time difference made it even harder to stay connected. "I was used to talking to them every day," she said. "But now it's really hard to catch them. The single ones leave their offices and go to the gym and then go out, and my married sons go home to their wives and kids. And that's especially tricky because of course I'm dying to see my grandchildren, but you don't want to be the mother-in-law who calls all the time."

Lydia realized that with her sons now grown and leading their lives, she would need to find new ways to occupy herself. She threw herself into work and made a concerted effort to reach out to her friends and make plans—dinners, tennis matches, trips to the museum. "When your kids are finally gone, you kind of have to sit down and say, 'Now what?'" she told me. "And I'm still figuring out the answer. Kids bring so much energy into your life—different people and all sorts of new experiences and ideas. When you get older, you have to generate that energy yourself, and you have to work at it. It's very hard."

> *Kids bring so much energy into your life—different people and all sorts of new experiences and ideas. When you get older, you have to generate that energy yourself, and you have to work at it.*

Another friend of mine, Evie, had similar feelings when her youngest daughter started thinking about college. "It surprised me how reluctant I was to let her go," she told me. "With the first one, Margaret, it didn't affect me quite so much, because she was always more independent. But Katie was my baby. I felt like when she was gone, my job as a mother would be over. Of course I wanted her to go to college and be successful and be happy, but I had a lot of very mixed emotions."

When Katie began visiting colleges, she decided that her first choice of schools was a small liberal arts college in the Midwest—much to Evie's dismay. "I would have so much preferred that she stay on the East Coast where she'd be only a train ride away," she recalled. "But Katie was fixated on this school. We went to look at it, and sure enough, a few weeks later she got a card in the mail that said, 'Would you like to apply early decision?' And her mind was set. She applied and got in, but the funny thing was that the school also sent *me* an acceptance letter by mistake. I guess there had been some clerical mix-up. My husband, of course, thought this was hilarious. He knew how I was feeling about the entire thing." She laughed, saying, "When I called the admissions office to let them know, I said, 'Katie is coming, and we'll be sad to see her go, but I draw the line at going back to college so I can be close to my daughter!'"

My friend Cory and her husband have two children and she said, "Everybody says it goes by so fast, but you're having such a good time with them that you don't realize what's happening until all of a sudden, that empty nest comes. Before you know it, they're off on their own and independent, but you're so used to being involved in every part of their lives, consulted on every decision, that when all that changes, it can be tough. And then there are wives and girlfriends and boyfriends and husbands in the middle and they drive the decisions now, and that's as it should be. But it's hard to step back and realize that your role has changed. The hardest part is losing control."

On the other hand this can be a time of real liberation because now that your children can take care of themselves, you are free to pursue your own interests. My friend Jean was telling me the other day about how she bumped into her friend Marjorie on the street. They were chitchatting, and before long Jean asked her, "How's your daughter?" To Jean's surprise, Marjorie replied, "You know, I haven't talked to her in a couple of weeks, I've just been so busy. But we're having lunch next Tuesday."

"This really struck me," Jean recalled, "because with so many of the older women I know, the news in their lives is usually about the children—you always get all the latest details about who's getting married, who's having a baby, who's buying a house, who's changing jobs. But this woman had so much going on that she didn't even know what her children were up to! She had been hiking in Switzerland and doing literacy work and was busy writing an article for some magazine. It was obvious that she kept her life very, very full."

We got the news that Renny would be deployed to Al Anbar province in Iraq in the spring of 2006. I had been dreading this call from the moment three years earlier when he'd first told me he was joining the Marines. I was terrified, but I didn't want him to know it. I told him I was fine and made him promise to e-mail me whenever he could so that I'd know he was okay.

Renny would be in Al Anbar for seven months, and during that time, I really struggled to keep it together. If we hadn't heard word in four or five days, I was a wreck. We knew where he was most of the time, but sometimes we didn't and he'd write us afterward and tell us that he'd been with the governor of Al Anbar in Ramadi. There were many, many attempts on the governor's life during that time, so this sort of thing just made my hair stand on end. Steve coped with all of this by reading all the newspapers and watching television and talking to people about it, but I couldn't listen to the news and asked people not to bring it up. I really put my head in the sand, but it allowed me to get through the day. Steve also had two other children that he could call when we didn't hear from Renny, and that would make me crazy because he had somewhere else to go while I had nowhere—Renny was my only child. Instead, I would go into the bathtub and sob.

My friends were wonderful during this time. They would call me to go to lunch or take a walk or play golf, and I will never forget those people who reached out. I would go and listen to what was going on with my friends' children or grandchildren and it definitely helped me to be interested in what they were do-ing . . . until I remembered that my son was out in 110 degree weather in the Iraqi desert. There were also very good friends who would call up and ask me perfectly innocent questions like, "Did you hear that they are bombing in Al Anbar? Isn't that where Renny is?" I found these questions excruciating. I mean, OF COURSE we knew that they were bombing, but I was doing whatever I could to avoid thinking about it. I would have to tell these people, "Please don't talk about it," as doing so only brought horrible visions into my head.

One time Steve and I were at a large dinner party at a friend's apartment and the hostess was telling us about their son Todd who had recently broken his leg skiing. She laughingly said, "Oh, here we were, worried about Renny, and it's Todd who gets hurt." Well, I almost walked out of the dinner. I said to Steve later, "What in God's name was she thinking? How could she possibly equate the two of them—Todd skiing with his friends and Renny in Iraq being bombed?" I was extremely sensitive at this time and while I know my friend was just making conversation, I couldn't bear to hear it.

During those long months that Renny was overseas, what gnawed at me the most was the fact that he had CHOSEN to put himself in danger. REAL danger. This was not some catastrophe of happenstance or bad luck, this was the path he had opted to take. Every time I opened my closet door and saw that pair of well-worn green espadrilles sitting there, I felt the pain of know-ing that he wasn't my little boy anymore. And I knew that this was my ultimate test as a parent—to support him as an equal, as an adult, regardless of whatever fear or heartache I felt so that he could live the life he wanted.

> *And I knew that this was my ulti-mate test as a parent—to support him as an equal, as an adult, regardless of whatever fear or heartache I felt so that he could live the life he wanted.*

Finally the day came when Renny returned from Iraq. I tried not to let my heart get too excited right up until the moment I saw him, for fear that something would happen and he'd be snatched away again. But suddenly there he was in front of me, looking even taller and stronger than I'd remembered, and words can't begin to express the joy I felt. We gave him a party to welcome him home, and he stood up in front of all the guests and told us in a toast how much it had meant to him that Steve and I had stood by his decision.

SEMPER FI. Always Faithful.

Later that night, after everyone had gone home, Renny and I were sitting together, drinking coffee in our living room. He said to me, "You know, Mom, as a Marine officer, you go out in front into the unknown and you don't know what's going to happen. But you go anyway because you know that if you don't, no one else will be able to get through. You always told me to live my own life, to find out who I was, and to stay true to what I believed in. I did, and I just wanted to thank you for that. Mom, you are the one who is out in front for me."

Even though our children may be grown and independent, there are still countless joys to be had with family during our later years. One of the best perks of growing older is being able to watch a whole NEW crop of family coming into the world. Steve and I now have four grandchildren through his children, Genie and Sandy, and these marvelous little people have allowed us to reexperience much of the fun of parenting—without the dreaded midnight feedings and diaper changes. It will never be the same as those years I had with Renny, but watching them scamper around our apartment or gush over the penguins at the Central Park Zoo definitely takes me back, and in some small way, makes me feel young again. If they're coming to visit, I have oodles of fun planning activities and making sure that we have spaghetti and PB&J on hand, or whatever else it is that they're eating these days. I want to do everything for them because that impulse is still there. When Renny has a child, I'm sure I'll be one of those grandmothers who wants to be around their grandchildren all the time (although I probably won't be allowed to be).

Even Steve went through a rather remarkable metamorphosis when our first two grandchildren, Jack and Eliza, arrived. Steve is one of the most active men around—he works all day, goes out to dinner at night, exercises, plays golf, and barely stops to rest. But for Jack and Eliza, he would stop all of these activities at the drop of a hat. He would even sit STILL. As his wife of thirty-five years, I would look on in amazement while he played cars and trucks for hours with Jack, or sat with Eliza while she watched the same *Sesame Street* movie over and over. Jack cleverly looks a lot like his grandad, and Eliza is so cute that she doesn't have to resemble anyone but herself, and our other two grandchildren, Ashlyn and Alexa, are equally adorable and perfect. From the moment each one of them arrived, Steve was wrapped around their little fingers. He once drove four hours in a snowstorm to take Jack sledding. He will lie down on the ground so Ashlyn and Alexa can jump all over him. He has even, heaven forbid, passed up a round of golf to watch them splash in the water at the beach. And the best part is that Grandad enjoys it all as much as they do.

The grandchildren come to our apartment and we let them play in all the rooms and jump on the couches and make all sorts of messes, and I think messes are wonderful things. Just like the time when Renny and I threw pies at each other on the beach. As we get older, we get used to having everything just so, but when you have grandchildren around I think you have to make a decision to let it go—otherwise you'll end up missing out.

My friend Cynthia, who lives in Portland, Oregon, came back east to visit her parents in New York City for Christmas one year. She came over to our apartment when we had Genie and Sandy, their spouses, and the four grandchildren as well as Renny staying with us for the holidays. There were blow-up air mattresses all over the house and toys all over the place, and she walked in and said, "I have to leave. I can't stand the chaos. How do you do it?" And I explained to her, "You know, it doesn't bother me. It's not worth it to me to lose their love over a messy room." Nor do I want to spend time worrying about whether or not they're saying "please" and "thank you" or putting their napkins in their laps. They're only children after all. Once, when Renny was a toddler, he hollered, "I'm taking 'peas' and 'gangu' and throwing them out the window!" And he walked over to the window and pretended to throw them out. I don't know who was riding him about "please" and "thank you," maybe it was Steve or the nanny, but I thought it was absolutely hysterical.

Of course, when you're talking purely about stamina, one can definitely be run ragged by grandchildren. My friend Christine and I were practically undone after a day of taking care of a friend's granddaughter, who I call Perfect Emily. Emily was two and a half with huge blue eyes, fabulous dimples, and very blond hair. Her family had asked us to watch her for the day while they took Emily's father to have an operation.

When I arrived at Emily's house at nine A.M., Chris opened the door, already looking exhausted. She had been there since six thirty A.M. and she had been down on the floor for several hours alternately playing the wind, a monster, the clouds, and the doctor.

We decided to take Perfect Emily, who was in no way tired, to visit seven Labrador puppies who were five weeks old. Well, we'd both forgotten what a production it is to go anywhere with a toddler. You need to bring the portable potty, extra clothes, sippy cups, toys, and the car seat. It took us about twenty minutes to get underway. Of course, she needed to go to the bathroom the minute we started off. We stopped the car and pulled out the potty, grateful that there were two of us to handle one thirty-pound girl. Naturally, there was a change of mind, and the potty was put back in the car empty. We started off again.

Arriving at the puppies' house, we disembarked. Several toy stuffed animals joined us as we marched into the house. The puppies adored Emily, as she was just their size. They bounded all over her, licking, sniffing, nipping . . . and the nipping didn't go down so well. Suddenly, Emily, who had been up since six A.M., realized that it was lunchtime. This entailed putting everything back into the car and heading back to her house. When we got there, we served her lunch exactly as her mother had told us to do. I cut up her turkey into pieces—too small, as it turns out—but Emily graciously ate them anyway.

After lunch we knew it was nap time—PRAYED it was nap time—but first we needed to get down on the floor and play mommy and daddy and baby puppies. We were so exhausted we could hardly stand, and when we tottered up, Emily needed to get her spotted doggie stuffed animal that had been left in the car. Out we went, and then we had to play car. This meant pretending eighty-eight times that we were going very fast to the grocery store, bouncing up and down and jiggling. Somehow, during all this, Emily managed to put several coins into the seat belt lock, which meant we had to spend half an hour getting the coins out. How could she still be going, we wondered, the dimples still dimpling, the eyes bluer than ever? "Emily, nap time," we insisted. Looking us straight in the eyes, she replied, "My mommy doesn't like me to take naps." Absolutely perfect delivery. I believed her instantly, even though her mother had told us about her daily naps and stressed their importance. But she was so enchanting that we naturally acknowledged her right to stay up. Here her mother had entrusted her child to our care, two intelligent, fifty-something women, both mothers ourselves, and we had become completely unraveled by two dimples.

Obviously we all love grandchildren because they represent the new beginnings in life. And to witness the beginnings again is wonderful, especially when our own lives now sometimes feel like they have more endings than anything else. I had a chance to witness these new beginnings just a little while ago when I found all three of my granddaughters going through my shoe closet. I was in the kitchen and suddenly the house became very quiet—which, as any parent knows is the first sign of danger when children are about. I went from room to room until I found them in my bedroom and there they were, each one trying on a different pair of shoes and trying, unsuccessfully I might add, to walk in them. It was at that moment that I realized I wasn't the only one getting ready to change my shoes.

The Wisdom of Old Women: Shut Up Unless You're Asked for It

One evening recently, when Renny was at home, he was heading out after dinner to meet up with some friends. It was early autumn but the weather was already turning cool, and as he was going out the door, I called to him, "Renny, it's cold out. Don't forget your sweater!"

"Mom," he said, fixing me with a solid gaze, "I just came back from Iraq. I can really figure out on my own if I need a sweater."

He was right, of course. But I couldn't help it. It just bubbles out, the mothering and the advice. But at this point in our lives, I truly believe that we need to give our children the credit that they deserve. They might just be able to take care of themselves after all.

When I was younger, I loved spending time with my Aunt Ano—my mother's sister—and now that I look back, it was largely because she was always so interested in ME. She could have had an affair that day with seventeen men or won the lottery and I wouldn't have known it. She never talked about herself or offered unsolicited opinions or suggestions. Instead, she would say, "Tell me what's happening. How's Renny? How are your mother and father? How's Steve?" She was so interested in my life that I loved her. And to this day I miss her terribly.

Taking an interest in young people is the key to keeping them in our lives without holding them hostage to the past.

Showing a genuine interest in them without being judgmental or talking about yourself will keep them coming back to you. I enjoy listening to young people talk about their marriages and babies and professional achievements because that is LIFE, and they are right smack in the middle of it. No one cares that I used to be on a soap opera, or maybe they do, but I'm not going to be the one to bring it up.

Whenever I see my friends' children at a wedding or a party, I love to chat with them for a bit—just for a little while, because I don't want to impose, and they're usually busy flirting or partying or trying to do their thing, whatever it is. But they're FUN and I derive such energy from being around them. I'll try to avoid the boring questions like, "How's the baby doing?" and ask something REAL, like, "How are you getting along with your husband? Is the baby interfering or is he adding to your relationship?" and they like that. A lot of my friends will say, "My kids love you," and I know it's because I ask them these kinds of questions.

Of course we all fall into the trap of making small talk, even with our own children. Renny is now in graduate school, and when I see him I'll inevitably ask him, "How are your classes?" And do I care? Maybe a little, but I really want to know what he's thinking and feeling. But if I say, "Renny, what are you thinking and feeling?" he'll say, "Mom, about what?" Well, life? That's the kind of thing you want to share, and it's often hard to bridge that gap of years and generations. But we have to try, and setting aside our role as the parent and listening to them, person to person, adult to adult, is a great first step.

CHAPTER SIX

Acts of Mercy

*W*hen I was first starting out as an actress in New York, I had lunch with my father every Friday at a restaurant named Jason's on Madison Avenue. Unlike my mother, who was generally disdainful of my efforts, my father loved hearing about my work. We would order steak frites and I would tell him about my auditions, or regale him with the details of what it was like to shoot a commercial, with everyone fussing over you as though you were a Barbie doll and the camera zooming right in close the entire time. My father always joked that his office colleagues, who were usually seated a few tables over, must be wondering why he was having lunch with such a beautiful young woman. They didn't know I was his daughter—and I don't think he ever told them, either!

When I was growing up, my father was the strong, steady force in our family; he was gentle and calm and levelheaded, and his friends always said he was the salt of the earth. He worked as a lawyer for Caltex (California Texas Oil Company) and often traveled to the Middle East, and my brother, sister, and I used to speculate (only half-kiddingly) that he also worked for the CIA. He had been in the Navy during World War II and would often go down to Washington, D.C., whenever he returned from Saudi Arabia. When I was in my teens, he was often gone for months at a time, and we used to wonder what he was doing then as he'd never traveled for such long stretches at any other point in our lives. He parented the three of us in a watchful but never over-bearing way; he knew how to make me ASK for his insights in life, rather than offering them to me unsolicited. Many years later, when he caught my niece Meg smoking in a café with her friends, he said nothing . . . but later that night, he told her a funny story about how he happened to stop smoking and how hard it was. He handled it beautifully by relating to her rather than scolding her, which was exactly how he had approached us when we were young.

My mother, on the other hand, was the complete opposite. Whereas Daddy was very stable and grounded, she was dramatic and glamorous and highly emotional. She was also exceptionally beautiful, and I had more than one boyfriend during high school who said to me, "I hope you look like your mother when you get to be her age." In truth, I looked a lot more like my father (all three of us did) and my mother never tired of telling me what a shame it was that I didn't look more like her. Looks were very important to her as they had been her ticket in life, and one of the ways she related to us was by constantly critiquing our hair or clothes, as well as the other choices we made. This bothered me, of course, but from a very early age I was quite independent and would do my own thing regardless of what she or anyone else thought. She called me her gypsy, and always said (not without some amount of pride) that I "marched to a different drummer."

But there was also another side to my mother, one that was softer and more nurturing and loved us, her three children and her husband. When I was little, she took me to museums to see exquisite Fabergé eggs and Chinese scrolls, and to parks and botanical gardens to learn about and delight in flowers, which she adored. When I was older, we would go out for lunch at a restaurant that served waffles all day and had a working cuckoo clock, and I treasured those afternoons together when it was just the two of us. She loved to read and would often drop a book by my room; it was her way of talking to me. And she could also be incredibly understanding: When a friend of mine died during high school, she was there in a second, helping me cope with the shock and the grief, and when I got my heart badly broken in college, she knew exactly what I was going through and was there again to help me pick up the pieces.

My mother was also something of a free spirit, imaginative and inventive, and for most of her life, I think she was torn between her deep-seated need to follow the rules and an equally passionate desire to break them. She was adamant about social conventions and proper upbringing, and yet she would often say to us, "I don't care what everyone else does, and I don't care what anyone else says—you have to be true to yourself." Interestingly, when this backfired on her and I embraced her motto and grew up to be an actress, she was horrified. My sister, Margo, was always her favorite because, unlike me, she was the good girl who did as she was told and willingly followed in my mother's footsteps; she grew up and got married and had the right kind of house in the right neighborhood, and had the children and the station wagon, exactly as my mother had prescribed.

I suspect that deep down, my mother was envious of my independence and the fact that I had been brave enough to choose a different path—one that she herself might have chosen had she been born into a different generation—and that this accounted for her sometimes-harsh criticisms of me. She herself had wanted to be an actress, but could never get past the thought that acting was "déclassé." She had spent all those years at home with us while my father went off and traveled the world, and I think she would have preferred to be traveling, too; she wanted adventure, and HE was the one having it, and this caused discord between them from time to time. In fact, many years later, when Steve, Renny, and I traveled with my parents to Morocco for their seventieth birthdays, I was delighted to see that my mother was absolutely in her element. Here we were, thousands of miles away from her quiet suburban enclave, finding our way in a new and rather difficult place, and she was thriving. I've often wondered what else she might have done with her life if she hadn't been constrained by the expectations of her time.

My friend Clarice once observed (somewhat wryly) that the bonds that exist within a family are like little tentacles that pull you in, and that you can never break free entirely, no matter what you do. On *Guiding Light*, this was certainly true, as year after year, those five intertwined families clung to one another and continued to be a part of each other's lives despite the drama and heartache. My own family was certainly no different. We had our ups and downs, but I loved my parents and accepted them as they were, even though my mother could be challenging. And as they got older and began needing more from me, there was no way I was going to let them down.

They say that we become our parents' parents in the end, or as Wordsworth wrote, "The child is father of the man." For me, the darkest, most difficult part of aging was watching my parents grow old and slip away. Nothing quite prepares you for the unsettling feeling of being called upon to care for those who once cared for you, or of seeing the two people who brought you into this world take their leave. It tests you, and when I was caring for my parents in their final years, there were times when the stress and strain were so great that I wasn't sure I could go on. But that is what being a family is all about: If you love one another, if you honor each other, you don't leave when things get tough. This

> *Nothing quite prepares you for the unsettling feeling of being called upon to care for those who once cared for you.*

was one of the greatest gifts my parents gave me: They never gave up on each other or on our family, and now that they were growing old, I wouldn't give up or walk away from them.

My mother's behavior first started to change when she was eighty-four. She had always been a whirlwind of energy, but now she seemed to be taking a lot of naps—and at first we wondered if her martinis and aperitifs had become too much for her. So we started to monitor her drinking and everything seemed to be normal. But as time went on, it became clear that something else was amiss, and she sensed it, too. One day when we were out shopping together and in the middle of a busy store, she suddenly grabbed my arm and looked me dead in the eye and said, "There's something very wrong with me." But when I pressed her about it, she just smiled and waved it off.

When we took her to the doctor, he confirmed our suspicions: She had been having little strokes and we were witnessing the first signs of senility. He couldn't say for sure how quickly her illness would progress, but there was nothing we could do about it other than take care of her and watch for any sudden changes. My father took her home, determined to continue on just as they always had, and I left the doctor's office feeling frightened of what the future might possibly hold.

With each passing month, my mother had more strokes and retreated further and further into her dementia. It was sad and terrifying and irritating all at once. She would hide her jewelry and blame the gardener for stealing it (when in fact they hadn't had a gardener for many years), or take the silver to the vault with my father and then insist it was stolen, too, even when he would tell her where it was. She bragged incessantly to her friends that my brother was running for governor of New York and that she was throwing him a huge party in Central Park, and people really believed her—and would ask me whether I thought he could win. She started wearing little berets and was just as lovely looking as she'd ever been, but the minute she spoke people knew something was wrong. She would try hard to follow the conversation around her and make appropriate responses, which were usually so far off that they were either very sad or very funny. She would ask her friends, "How are the children?" and they would answer happily, thrilled to tell her their latest news . . . until they realized that she hadn't taken any of it in. My mother would just smile benignly and ask, "How are the children?" again, ignorant of the long exposition that had taken place.

The only blessing in this situation was that my mother didn't know what was happening to her. On the contrary, she was in her own happy world. In the middle of a family dinner, she would whisper, "Tina, I have a secret to tell you. I sang 'The Star-Spangled Banner' last night at Yankee Stadium, right in the middle of the field, and I remembered all the words and everyone loved me. They applauded and applauded. I was a hit!" This gave her no small amount of pleasure, and in some ways, her new childlike demeanor made her easier to be around. My once-caustic mother, who had always told me I was too heavy or too thin, my hair too long or too short, or my skirts too long or too short, was now walking down the street beside me, holding my hand, and praising me to the skies. "Tina, it is just so good to spend time with you, my dear!" Dementia had made her a much sweeter person.

My friends found her senility charming, and two of my closest friends, Corny and Terry, would come to lunch with me and my parents and dote on my mother and make her feel special. We would go to a nearby restaurant where my mother would order soup, finish it, and then suggest that we order soup. Corny would tell her that she'd already had the soup, and my mother would ask if she had liked it. When Corny said yes, she'd beam at her indulgently. Corny would also take my mother's gin martinis, which were very strong, and pour half of them into her own water glass. One time, forgetting her attempts to keep my mother from inebriation, she took an enormous gulp of water and turned ghostly white, realizing that she had just taken a huge gulp of gin by mistake.

As time went on, most of my mother's own friends drifted away. The bridge games and luncheons ended, since when she was occasionally invited, she would forget to go. My mother had always thrived on attention and would speak of her "legions" of friends, but of course they had stopped calling as she no longer knew who they were. She was left with only remnants of her former self, like a sachet that has lost its fragrance after being left too long in a drawer.

My father coped with all of this admirably, and treated my

mother with deference and kindness, but he had to deal with the day-to-day extinction of my mother's personality, which was heartbreaking. And then we got the news that he had developed blood and bone cancer. He never complained and faced his diagnosis with incredible dignity, but he, who had once been the kindest man in the world, now became extremely demanding. "Tina! For God's sake, your mother needs some help this morning! She doesn't have any clothes that fit. You have to take her shopping!" Thus, where my mother had morphed into an angelic child, my father became a tyrant.

Suddenly, these two previously independent people had become mind-bogglingly reliant on me. Phone calls would come every morning: "There's no food in the house." "Your mother needs soap." "I have a doctor's appointment today and who's going to drive me?" Despite the fact that they already had full-time help at home, these questions rained down on me every day. I mean, I had a son, a husband, and a job, and now I had to worry about buying my mother underwear and making sure that she didn't wander out of the house when no one was watching. I felt sad and angry and protective and overwhelmed all at the same time. But my sister had died when she was in her forties and my brother was busy with his own life, so if I didn't step up, no one else was going to. Regardless of what I would have wished for if given a choice, their entire welfare and caretaking fell to me.

When I was young, my brother, sister, and I went to church with my parents every Sunday. We were raised Catholic and much of what the Church taught us remains with me until this day. I've always believed in the Acts of Mercy: Feed the hungry, give drink to the thirsty, clothe the naked, shelter the homeless, comfort the imprisoned, visit the sick, and bury the dead. So when someone close to me is sick or in the hospital, I go to see them even if I'm busy or would rather be doing something else (and like everyone, I would much rather be doing something else). When there's a funeral, I go and hope I can be of some comfort. We all do these things because they are essential to us as human beings. And for this reason, and many personal ones, I believed very strongly that taking care of my parents in the last years of their lives was something I had to do, and that I would do it as best I could, no matter what.

It didn't take long for me to realize that they needed more help than the caregiver and I could give them. I had finally taken away my father's car keys and while doing so was an absolute necessity, it had made them even more dependent on me than they were before. My father had desperately tried to resist, making excuses, saying that he might have to drive my mother to the hospital in the middle of the night. But he was in his eighties and his vision was terrible and he liked a martini at lunch (sometimes two), so it was terrifying to think of him on the road. I pleaded with him until he ultimately agreed to hand over the keys, but he still kept the car in the garage. It sat there for such a long time, like a sad, empty shell. It was so hard for him—driving symbolized freedom and autonomy, and now both of those were slipping from his grasp.

After an agonizing debate with my husband, I decided that they needed to move to an assisted-living facility where they could have help and be looked after around the clock. But no one had told me that it's nearly impossible to get someone into assisted living if they are already suffering from dementia, which my mother most certainly was. You have to apply early when you're still fit and able, and my parents had never made or even contemplated any arrangements of this kind. To make matters worse, when I suggested assisted living, my father was adamant that they didn't want to go. I finally broke down in tears and told him that he was being selfish and that I was exhausted running out to the suburbs every day when he called and ordered me to do something. He finally grasped the difficulty of my situation and said begrudgingly that they would go.

We found a place that was lovely and quite close to New York City so I would still be able to get out and see them on a regular basis. I begged, charmed, and cajoled the director of the home and when we went for the interview, my mother just sat there silently and smiled, which was exactly what we needed her to do. Of course as soon as my parents were living there, the staff realized how "forgetful" she was, but my father was still so bright and on top of things despite his illness that he made up for it. He took care of everything for the both of them and tended to my mother, which gave me some peace of mind.

Once they were settled in their new home, I drove out to see them whenever I could. These visits could be both heartening and discouraging. The facility itself was lovely, with wonderful food and expansive gardens for strolling that were filled with the flowers my mother loved. My mother kept thinking it was my house: "Oh, Tina, your new house is just beautiful. Was it expensive? I love the way you've decorated, darling. The movies must pay you so well. You look just beautiful. You're my star."

And then moments later: "Who are you?"

"Tina, Mom, I'm Tina."

Every Saturday, I would go out to see them and we'd have lunch together and watch a movie in their room. My mother would always say, "I want to watch *Sister Act*. You know, that movie with the funny black woman. I love her." Whenever I pointed out that she'd seen *Sister Act* a hundred times, she'd say, "What are you talking about? I've never seen *Sister Act* in my life."

So of course, we would watch *Sister Act*. Every time we saw it was the first time for my mother, and she would howl with laughter at jokes I had heard too many times to count. My father laughed, too, seeing her enjoy it, so I didn't mind watching it over and over. I'd sit there between them, the two of them laughing, and my mother adding in strange little asides, fantastical things like *"I think I'm a nun."* My father would just smile at her as though she'd said the most brilliant thing in the world.

But when it came to me, my father remained extremely difficult. As his disease progressed, he was in so much pain that he couldn't help taking it out on me. "Damn it, Tina, you've got to make an appointment for your mother to have her hair done! You need to rearrange this room as I keep bumping into the coffee table! And I need some new sweaters, these woolly ones hurt my skin." He was so angry about everything, mostly that he was dying. There was a psychiatrist at the facility who told me that it is common for patients to take out their frustration and fear on their caregivers. Of course my father never yelled at the nurses; he'd kid around with them, and he couldn't yell at my mother because she didn't even know who she was. But I was safe to yell at so I bore the full force of his rage. Plus, I now had control of their finances and this was very, very hard for him to accept. Finally, I had to have the psychiatrist talk to my father to tell him, "You cannot keep doing this to your daughter. It is unfair to her and you will lose her." I didn't want to keep coming to visit and being abused. After that, for the most part, my father was better. He knew he was lashing out at me for being young and alive, but he couldn't help himself.

Meanwhile, I'd also discovered that the rest of their affairs were in a state of total disarray. My father had been a tax lawyer for Caltex, and yet he was completely disorganized when it came to his own estate. I found out that he had left everything to my mother—a scary choice since she would probably run out and spend the money on a Ferrari, or throw my brother that party in Central Park, or just give the money to the first person who strolled past her. And then there was the house to deal with. I had to go through all their furniture and belongings, and divide them up between myself and my brother and my sister's daughter, and then—since assisted living doesn't come cheap and my parents had never taken out any sort of long-term-care insurance—I had to sell their house to pay for their nursing facilities, which over time, cost them nearly all their assets. I spent hours upon hours calling and meeting with lawyers and accountants and doctors, and it took everything I had to keep wading through this quagmire of wills and old taxes and medical forms and property deeds. Part of me was furious that all of this had fallen on me, but I couldn't truly be angry because, as my father said, he'd thought he'd be dead at seventy-five. He never thought he'd live to be in his nineties—and in the generations that came before him, no one ever did.

My parents needed so much, and there was no one else to do it but me. You know that a newborn baby is going to be helpless, but you don't anticipate this from the people who always guided you. I took care of their wills, I took care of their bills, I took care of their clothes, I even moved my sister from the grave she was in because my father said he'd like for Margo to be next to them in the cemetery when they died. You name it, and I did it. And it became like an obsession. Taking care of my parents consumed everything in my life: Renny was away at college by this point, but my career and my marriage definitely took a backseat.

Every spare minute I had, I rushed up to see them, to bring my mother lavender bubble bath or macaroons or whatever else she wanted, and to be sure that they were being cared for properly and hadn't taken a turn for the worse.

I think a part of me believed that by doing these things— bringing them the right soap or their favorite cookies, making them smile and be happy, even if only for a moment—I could fix them and bring them back to the way they once were. But we can't fix our parents when they reach the endgame of aging, and this is our greatest sadness. Still, we keep trying if only for that fleeting instant when they laugh, or take pleasure in the flowers we've brought, or seem alert and joyful again. In that moment, we forget the pain of watching them disappear, and we feel like we are THEIR children again, instead of the other way around.

Not surprisingly, the stress of caring for my parents began to take a serious toll. I hated them one minute and loved them mightily the next, and as time went on I fell into a depression that I couldn't shake. The days I spent with them were filled with a thousand small indignities, from buying my mother her first package of Depends, to enduring my father's fits of anger, to hearing him say later on, his voice breaking, "We don't belong here." I would cry a lot after visiting them and sometimes I would walk away thinking, "Oh God, I can't get through it. I can't go back there. I can't stand it." But then I'd get home and think, "Oh, the poor things, they're up there alone, they need to see me." And it was agonizing to know this. So, a few days later, I'd go back.

The low point came one day when I was pushing both my parents in wheelchairs along a narrow precipice near the hospital. I was taking my father to the doctor, and he had insisted that my mother come along—he hated to leave her alone even for a minute, and with good reason, since he was the only person she still recognized. I was wheeling them side by side down this rather steep incline, and I was afraid that at any moment I would lose my grip and one of them would get away from me. My father was shouting at me to be careful of him because he was in so much pain, and my mother kept turning around to ask me, "And who are you, dear?" and they were both just so far out at this point that I didn't think I could bear it for one second longer.

And then I started laughing. The horror of the situation—mine and theirs—suddenly struck me as very funny. And then I started crying. I just totally lost it. I continued pushing them along with tears running down my face, laughing and crying until a nice young man saw that I was having trouble and offered to help. Together we somehow got them into the doctor's office, where I begged the doctor to admit my father to the hospital as he was in such pain. But my father didn't want to leave my mother, and so he hung on day after day, week after week, right by her side, refusing to go anywhere, and all I could do was be there and try to help.

During this time, which lasted for close to five years, I didn't have it in me to care about what shoes I was wearing one way or the other. In fact, most days I didn't even feel like getting out of bed. But when I did, I moped around in my bunny slippers or, if I had to leave the house, I usually wore the same pair of scuffed and broken-in black flats and they looked very much like the shoes of defeat. The world around me seemed to be falling apart: Renny was on his way to Iraq and Lillian's role on the show was fading, and my parents were dying, and I just couldn't see a way out. But I knew that I had to keep putting one foot in front of the other. I had given my life over to caring for my parents and was getting no thanks or appreciation for it, but I HAD to do it. I wanted to do it. It was my duty. And I would see it through to the end.

My husband, Steve, comes from a classic WASP family and from the moment he introduced me to them so many years ago, I always stood out as the dramatic, emotional one (rather like my mother in her day). As a rule, WASPs are skilled at sublimating any emotion, and in the face of disaster, they will stoically continue on as though nothing whatsoever has happened. I am normally the antithesis of WASP behavior, but in those years that I was taking care of my parents, I became incredibly adept at tamping down the pain and soldiering on.

But there came a point when I realized that I was going to have to change my approach. Things with my parents were only going to get worse before the end, and if I continued on this way much longer, I wouldn't be able to help anyone, not even myself. I had to find a way to get even the tiniest amount of emotional distance from what was happening. Otherwise I would be swallowed by the anguish.

My brother, John, has always been the kind of person who can find humor in a dishwasher, and he had decided early on to find my mother hilarious. We'd be having lunch at the facility and my mother would order a martini, and when they brought her some cranberry juice instead, she'd say, "This is much too strong!" and send it back. I'd be absolutely crazed when she did these things, but John would be laughing, and I finally just decided, Why not laugh, too? I mean, WHY NOT? Why not see the humor in it? Because it was funny, even though it was horrifying.

As time went on, I learned to play along when she did these things, and it did make the pain easier to bear. When she complained that the staff had taken her jewelry (in her addled mind the jewelry was *constantly* being stolen), instead of saying, "No,

Mom, you're wrong," I'd say, "Okay, Mom, where do you think they hid it?" I'd play a game with her as if she were a little child. She would ask for my sister—"When is Margo coming?"—and rather than explain to her again that Margo had died, I would say, "Oh, she'll be here in a little while," which seemed to satisfy her. I played into her insanity, which not only made things easier for me, but seemed to make things easier for her as well. It also felt a lot like acting, and since I was acting less on the show, I started to act more in real life. I made my living as an actress, so why not defy death by acting as well?

I also tried to find ways to enjoy my mother and her new childlike persona. I brought her the *Eloise* books and the *Babar* books and the *Madeline* books that she had loved when we were kids, and we read them together and her eyes would light up. I brought her all of those funny Chevy Chase movies from the eighties, and she would howl with laughter watching him fall off the roof again and again while putting the lights up in *Christmas Vacation*. She was amused so easily, and once I'd accepted the fact that *Sister Act* was now more enjoyable for her than the sophisticated French films she'd once loved, I found ways that we could be together and actually have a good time.

I also found a good shrink who could listen to me and offer advice, and it was such a relief to have an outlet for the multitude of painful emotions that I was feeling. I went to her office twice a week and poured out my heart about everything from how little my father had weighed at my last visit, to how my mother could no longer dress herself, to how I sometimes wished that I lived in Fiji so my brother would have been stuck taking care of them— and I did it all without the slightest bit of self-consciousness or remorse because I had paid this woman to listen to me. I wasn't burdening Steve or my friends (all of whom had heard it again and again and must have been so fed up with my nonstop complaining). Just getting all the pent-up sadness and anger and frustration off my chest and out into the open in the shrink's safe office was liberating. Those feelings stayed with me, of course, but talking about them in a neutral setting took the edge off somehow and I found that I was better able to cope.

I also started to lean on my friends more. I had fallen out of touch with everyone when my parents moved to assisted living because I spent all my free time driving back and forth and getting them to their doctors' appointments and so on. Now when I felt like I needed the extra support, I'd ask one of them to come along with me for the day. I didn't ask them often, but they always said yes, and then afterward they would say, "My God, Tina, how do you do it?" And I would just look at them and say, "What option do I have?" The only other option was to wash my hands of them and flee.

I did flee once, but ONLY once, when my friend Anne and I decided to go on a trip to China. It was our shared birthday and we decided to escape and celebrate this big one for two weeks. Plus, I thought traveling would provide me with a much-needed break from everything I was dealing with back home. I was reluctant at first, because I worried about what would happen to my parents while I was away. They were both at a point where they could have been gone at any time. But Steve convinced me that I should go and when I left, I said to him, "Don't call me if they die. Don't even let me know, because there's nothing I can do." Of course when I came home they were alive. But from the minute I stepped on that plane, I forgot about my parents for what was the first time in years. There's something about changing your location that wipes the slate clean. And that trip was one of the things that saved me. I got away and took care of myself and when I returned, I no longer felt like I was going crazy.

My soap opera daughter, Beth Chamberlin, once told me that whenever she was going through difficult times, she just kept telling herself, "It's all material for acting." And it's true. When you're an actor, everything you go through becomes material that you draw upon for future roles. That's what life is all about—the beginnings, the endings, the joys, and the losses—and it is all worth experiencing, even the hard parts. We do learn something about ourselves when we are up against the wall, and we do most certainly come out stronger.

> *We do learn something about ourselves when we are up against the wall, and we do most certainly come out stronger.*

One Christmas, after Renny had come home from Iraq, we drove out to see my parents at the assisted living facility. We got in the car and snow started to fall, and by the time we got out there it had turned into a blizzard and the grounds and gardens were covered in white. We wheeled my parents into the solarium and we all just sat there watching the snow. Renny was shocked at how far they had deteriorated and how fragile they had become. When we left, he said to me in his usual wise way, "Enjoy them, Mom. They're not going to be here for very long."

One Saturday morning in late spring of the next year, I arrived at the home to visit my parents. My mother seemed much more aware than usual—she greeted me with enthusiasm and even remembered my name. "Tina, dear! It is so good to see you!" I sat down beside her and she continued, "I have the most wonderful idea, darling. Let's get dressed up and go out for a fancy dinner! I have the most wonderful dresses you can wear, and jewelry."

I was startled and delighted to see my mother so clearheaded. She knew who I was, and this was momentous for me. I took her dresses out of the closet, and I brought over her earrings for her to try on. Most of these dresses were now too small for her—my mother had always been a perfect size 6 but she had gained weight in recent years, as she would forget she had eaten, and eat again and again. I'd made sure that all her favorite dresses had come with her when they'd moved. We admired the dresses, and then she said, "You try on this one, darling. Aga gave me that dress."

"Aga?"

"You remember Aga, don't you? She and I were such good friends. We met when my father was stationed in Paris. The two of you were so alike, that's why I sent you to her all those years ago. I knew that she would understand you in ways I never could. Bring me those black satin shoes, would you?"

I brought her the shoes, and put on her makeup for her, and for the first time in so many years, my mother and I were perfectly happy together—talking and laughing and playing dress up.

And then she was gone again.

"Who are you?"

"I'm Tina, Mom."

It was a flicker . . . and then nothing.

My father died the next day, and my mother went right after him. No matter how long I'd been anticipating their deaths, it still seemed sudden. For the past five years they had been my entire life—and it had been this way because I loved them. And now they were gone.

At first the depression threatened to return. After I'd arranged the funerals and dealt with the details and seen my parents laid to rest, I went home and slept and slept and slept. I missed them terribly. I missed how my mother could smell a rose twenty-seven times and each time it would be new. I missed holding my father's hand as I sat between them in their room watching movies or listening to music or whatever else we'd done to pass the time. I just missed their beingness.

But soon another feeling began to creep in around the edges of my mind—one of relief. HUGE relief. And every day that feeling grew. After so many years of taking care of my parents, my life was my own once more. As I started the process of reclaiming my life, I felt a wonderful kind of peace—because I knew that I'd done everything for my parents that I possibly could.

Even now, my friends will still remark on how much I devoted myself to my parents during that time, how they don't know if they'd ever be able to do the same. But I think that for most of us, our sense of duty prevails, even if love doesn't. It comes down to those tentacles. Except in the most grievous of circumstances, nothing is going to win over family. Nothing.

As time went by, I began to consider what I had learned from my parents' final years. What lessons, if any, could I take away from everything that I—and they—had been through? What was the secret to living out the last years of your life in dignity and comfort? I now felt strongly that this was far more important than keeping away wrinkles or staying active in your professional life. After all, what good are makeup tricks and high-heeled shoes if you end up being a burden on your family—or worse, penniless and alone?

My parents had lived comfortably until the day they died, but the incredible expense of their housing and medical care had eaten away most of their estate, and I knew that my father would have undoubtedly preferred to leave something for his children. Plus, I'd had to devote so much of my life to sorting out their affairs. It's hard enough to watch your parents decline without also having to worry about where they are going to live,

> *What was the secret to living out the last years of your life in dignity and comfort?*

who will pay for their day-to-day care, what kind of care they will have, and all the associated legal paperwork. I knew without a doubt that I didn't want Renny to have to go through this with Steve and me. I wanted us to be prepared, both for our sakes and for his.

My friend Alina and I were discussing one day how "aging with grace" is often as simple as accepting the truth. And the truth is that we're not going to be here forever, and that we won't always be able to look after ourselves the way we do now. "I'm finally thinking seriously about moving back to Florida," Alina confided. Most of her family lived in Miami, and they had been encouraging her to return for some time. "I've been fighting it because I know that down there my primary role will be grandmother," she told me. "Whereas here I can work and do so many other things. But the reality is that I'm sixty-four, and my kids worry about me being all alone. They say, 'Mami, if something happens to you in your apartment, who's going to know?'" She laughed. "But there's some truth to it. I think there comes a time when you have to be honest with yourself."

She was right. And sadly, I had seen firsthand the results of poor planning, not just with my parents but with Aga—the woman I had always looked to as an example of a life well lived.

Several years after I saw her in Paris for the last time, I learned that one of the reasons she had become so feeble and diminished in her old age was that she had lost everything when her husband died. Her husband was English and a technicality did not allow him to leave his estate outside England. Everything he'd had was confiscated by the British government—the glorious apartment on Avenue Foch, the country house in Normandy—and Aga was left alone with nothing. She had been too proud to mention it when I saw her. Now, looking back, I couldn't help but wonder if better circumstances might have enabled her to retain her magic.

So I set about facing the truth of my own future, and gathering the information I needed—even though I would have preferred to be doing just about anything else under the sun. And NO, the process wasn't fun, or even interesting. It required sitting down with lawyers and doctors and accountants and asking unpleasant questions about money and health and wills. I had to sit on the telephone on hold, listening to horrible music, set up the appointments, and then sit in waiting rooms with old magazines . . . all of which culminated in having to endure dry, practical discussions about the future and "certain eventualities." I learned about Medicare and attended seminars on long-term-care insurance, and Steve and I spent hours discussing different scenarios. It took a lot of time, it cost me money, and above all it was so BORING. But I did it—even though I hated every minute—because I knew that I needed to have my affairs in order if I wanted the years ahead to be all that they could be.

And so, I bought a special pair of shoes that became my "taking care of business" shoes: cherry red flats that were a perfect blend of practicality and flair. They were the antidote to those horrid black flats that I had worn for so many years while I traipsed around from one doctor's appointment and one lawyer's office to the next, trying to find a way to help my parents. The red shoes were comfortable enough to wear on a day when I would be sitting through information sessions or walking long blocks between appointments, but whenever I looked down at my feet they made me smile. There was absolutely nothing defeated about them.

When I had finally taken care of everything, I felt that a weight had been lifted from my shoulders. I could now get on with the business of LIVING rather than worrying about what the future held. Even Renny seemed glad. After what I'd been through with my parents, I think he was relieved to know that we'd be looked after and that he wouldn't be responsible for making all the major decisions. Still, I know that he'll be there for us the minute we need him, ready to bring us underwear or bubble bath or whatever else will make us happy. Recently, when he described a new girlfriend to me, he said, "You know, Mom, she would take really good care of you when you get old." He's thinking about it. And that's really all that any mother can ask.

Legally Blonde

There's no denying that it's hideously boring to plan your estate. This fact, compounded by our natural fear of death, accounts for why such a shocking number of Baby Boomers have nothing in place for when they die. You'd be amazed at how many people give me a blank stare when I ask if they have a living will or long-term-care insurance. These are responsible, organized, professional types—many of whom have dependents relying on them—and they've done nothing to plan. If they were to go tomorrow, they'd leave behind a chaotic mess for their grieving loved ones to try to manage. And you need to plan ahead for your own sake as well—you can get so scared at the end that you don't always think clearly. That's why it's essential to do things calmly and rationally now. Here is a list of things to consider:

• *Where You Want to Live.* Be realistic about what you can manage as you get older. A three-story house is not easy to maintain so you are probably going to want to downsize to an apartment or condominium where most of the upkeep is managed for you. Beyond that, you will most likely need to consider assisted living or a nursing home. Go look at these places for yourself before it's a necessity—find the ones you like and get on a waiting list if necessary. This takes the burden off your family, and everyone will be happier to have a plan in place if and when it becomes time to go.

• *Your Will.* If you don't have one, get one. IMMEDIATELY. Find a good lawyer (ask people you trust for a recommendation), and have him or her walk you through the process. This is the ONLY way we can be absolutely sure that our wishes are carried out with regard to everything from money to personal property. Once your will is complete, make sure that everyone knows where you keep the copies.

• *Your Wishes for Medical Care.* Discuss your preferences with your children or spouse while you're healthy and create a liv-

ing will (different from your other will) so there is no con-
fusion later on. Specify what kinds of medical intervention
are okay, and when/if you would prefer to use a resource
like hospice. These questions can cause great strife among
families if they are not answered ahead of time, so now is
the time to get everyone on the same page.

• *Long-Term-Care Insurance.* Although the premium costs can
seem expensive if you're in perfect health, long-term-care
insurance can be a blessing if you wind up spending many
years in assisted living or a nursing home, as my parents did.
The bills pile up faster than you'd ever expect, and sometimes there is no end in sight. After my experience with my
mother and father, Steve and I both took out long-term-
care insurance so that we don't have to use all our money for
these expenses and can leave something for Renny, Genie,
and Sandy. It's a pile of money that's there for your use if
you need it, and it's an enormous relief to know that you're
covered. You can also investigate government subsidies for
nursing-home care—this may be another option.

• *Finances.* If you don't have an accountant or money manager
already, now is the time to get one. Diversify your holdings,
and be vigilant about following your portfolio and seeing a
paper trail. I personally think that it's best to avoid the aggres-
sive young stockbroker types who want to move your money
around constantly. The amount of risk we can afford varies
from person to person, but for my part, I want to be invested
in longer-range holdings at this point in my life.

• *Clutter Versus Heirlooms.* When you have to go through someone else's home, it's easy to mistake heirlooms for junk. You will save your loved ones a lot of time and energy (and possible regret) by clearing and weeding things out NOW. Throw the clutter and nonessentials away, and make a list of what in the house is important, either for sentimental reasons or because it's valuable. Even if you've told your son a hundred times why you love your father's eagle chest that's in the hallway, this is a chance to reiterate why it's significant for you. Remember to include anything that might be in storage. Then type up the list, give everyone a copy, and keep a copy with your wills. This is also a good time to specify who gets what: My brother, niece, and I divided up my parents' things before they died, so it was unemotional, and then we typed up the list, my father gave the okay, and there was no arguing about it after they were gone.

• *Memorials.* My mother-in-law had planned her whole funeral right down to the psalms and hymns, and we were so grateful to have everything in place. Steve and I have talked about who we want as ushers, and who would speak at our services, and we also have the deeds to our cemetery plots and other instructions about headstones and burial in our wills. As difficult as it might be to do this now, your family will thank you for it. You might also consider sitting down with a tape recorder and leaving a farewell message or writing letters to your friends and family now, when you can be calm and placid. You can remind listeners of little anecdotes so that the history isn't lost when you are gone. And tell them that you love them and try to give them some comfort. It's a wonderful gift for them and will help them through their periods of grief.

The WHEN List

I've spoken to many friends about their parents' deaths, and one thing that's clear is that you cannot wait until the end to let your heirs or spouse know where to find things. One friend's father left his life insurance in a trust that had been created decades before, but when he died his wife couldn't locate the paperwork. It will surely show up someday, probably in a spot that will seem a logical place to keep it, but in the meantime, his bereft wife spent weeks calling former lawyers of the family and finally had to appeal to a judge to gain access to the funds. It was agonizing. Don't let this happen to those you love!

I keep a file in the drawer of my desk, clearly marked, that contains all my major paperwork: my birth certificate, power of attorney, house deeds, and living will. It also includes a list I've made of my additional personal information such as bank accounts, insurance policies, investments, and so on, and where to find the relevant materials. I created this list so that if and WHEN someone ever needs this information and I'm not there to help, it's available in a clear and organized way.

Personal Affairs and Information
      Will—date, executors, location of, copies
      Lawyer, name and contact information

Birth date, place of birth
Marriage date, place of marriage

Personal Certificates

Birth, marriage, citizenship (if applicable)—location of, copies

Residences

For each residence, list the following:
  Address, including survey lot and plan number
  Ownership title in name of
  Conveyance papers
  Copies of bill of sale and deed, surveys, closing statement, building cost figures and/or alterations
  Insurance policy for property, name of insurance broker and contact info
  Property tax receipts

Insurance Policies

List location of brokers and contact information for all policies, including:
Life insurance, names of companies and contact information
Accident insurance, name of policies, agent and contact information. Note existence of extended coverages, i.e., nursing care, etc.
Hospital insurance number: Medicare, Medicaid, and other insurance numbers
Homeowners' insurance

Personal property insurance
Auto insurance

Bank Accounts
All accounts and account numbers, including safety
deposit boxes
Location of checkbooks, passbooks, bank cards
Accountant, name and contact information

Securities
Bond and stock certificates, location

Annuity Contracts
Name of policies, guaranteed periods, agents involved

Tax Returns
Location of copies of income tax returns

Charge Accounts
Names and numbers of all accounts

Record of Household Finances
Location

Employer
Address and telephone number

Funeral Arrangements
Name and location of funeral home, name of contact
there and contact's information

Cemetery Plot
> Name and location of cemetery, location of plots, date of purchase, location of deeds

Personal Property
> Location of jewelry and any items of particular note (silver, heirlooms, etc.)

And now—ON TO LIVING! BRAVA!

CHAPTER SEVEN

Breaking Through the Wall

About a year after Renny was born, my friend Kay invited me to join her for a morning run in Central Park. At the time, I was looking for a way to get back in shape, and even though I had never been a runner I agreed. Naturally I went out and bought the most incredible pair of bright yellow Saucony sneakers for the occasion (when I looked at them, they just made me feel like running), and we met on a bright, cold Sunday morning at eight A.M. at the park entrance at Seventy-second and Fifth. For the next twenty minutes we ran, huffing and puffing our way along various paths until we wound our way up to the Reservoir, a stunning body of water with panoramic views of the city skyline that occupies a full eighth of the park. Neither of us were in perfect shape—I'd had a baby a year before and we were not young physically (Kay's "baby" was seventeen). But we fell in step with the other joggers who were making their way around the Reservoir's 1.58 mile running track. We did half a loop and then called it a day—but we decided that we would meet at the same time next Sunday and see if we could make a habit of a weekly run.

For the rest of the week, I walked around the apartment in my pretty yellow running shoes. I loved wearing them; they made me want to move. When Steve asked me why I was wearing them all the time, I answered him breezily: "I'm going to run a marathon and I'm breaking them in." I had no idea why I said this—mostly I was just playing with him—but the little acorn was in the ground.

Before long, the word got out about Kay's and my new workout regimen, and some of our friends asked to join us on our little morning jogs. Soon there was a group of us gathering in the park on Sundays, all career women in our forties, with children. As we jogged we talked about what we wanted in life, how we intended to get it, our dreams, our men, our children, our disappointments—it was like free therapy and exercise all rolled into one. Before we knew it, we were running up to six miles a day, a fact which, when we discovered it, led to the question of whether, just perhaps, IT could be done.

I will never forget the morning IT first came up. We had just finished our jog and were standing around discussing the various activities that lay ahead of us that day, when out of nowhere I asked, "Why don't we run a marathon?" A part of me was kidding, but a part of me was dead serious. The whole group fell silent. I expected an uproar of excuses and raised eyebrows, and an outpouring of "How could you?" "What?" and "Are you kidding me?" But much to my surprise, no one said anything at all. We all just stood there looking at one another and actually contemplating this question. Then Kay started to laugh and we all started to giggle, so we said good-bye and went our separate ways. But for me, the gauntlet had been thrown down. The call was there, waiting for me to answer it. It seemed impossible, but somewhere inside I craved the challenge; I wanted to test myself to see if I could do it.

A week later, Kay and I decided to go for it. We knew that it was going to be tough, but the thrill of taking on the unknown spurred us on. We decided that we'd start with a half-marathon—thirteen miles—that was taking place in Brooklyn in five weeks' time. And then after that, MAYBE, just possibly, we'd try to take on the full New York City Marathon distance of 26 miles, 385 yards. It was daunting, but the courage of our years gave us stamina. We trained hard and went to Brooklyn and—amazingly—finished. By then we had the marathon bug. My yellow Saucony running shoes had started it all, and now it seemed they were going to pay the price as I ran and ran and ran.

Kay and I decided that rather than running the annual New York City Marathon, which seemed the obvious next step, we would aim for something that would really keep us motivated: We decided to run a marathon in Paris. If you only have one marathon in you—and I was sure that was all I had—why NOT do it in Paris? We would be running along the Seine, amid beautiful architecture, smelling the scent of the May flowers with gorgeous Frenchmen cheering us on. Paris—how easily that destination persuaded Kay to devote her vacation days and me to take time off from *Guiding Light*. At 26.2 miles, we would be spending far more than $26 a mile to get there, but a trip to the City of Light seemed like the best inspiration we could have.

And so, we began the grueling training process. This meant days of running alone, often in snow and rain. It meant juggling our one- to two-hour daily runs with careers, love, children, cooking, housework, and friends—which in turn meant either getting up very early or skipping lunch hour or arriving home too late for dinner. But we found that it could be done and we could do it. Besides, what was the alternative? Failure? Admit defeat? Never. Neither one of us was going to bring the other down—Kay and I were depending on each other to get through what we had started. Together, we could tolerate the boredom of the circling, the never-ending circling, of the Central Park Reservoir. We could arrive at work with aching shinbones, backs, and shoulders, and black toes and still make it through the day in reasonably good form. Central Park became our home away from home, and it was there, running mile after mile, that I discovered how mental discipline and physical discipline interrelate. I learned how to respect the self that persevered and frown upon the self that preferred to sleep late, bake brownies, and curl up with a good book.

I also discovered a new kind of female friendship, one that I had never experienced before. Until now, my friendships with women had been based on going to the movies, talking about "life," traveling together—all sorts of fun things. But running with a woman is different. I think men experience something similar on football fields where they face rigorous training and injuries to achieve a common goal. They tough it up and learn about spirit in combat. Kay and I learned about this spirit while running around the Reservoir, and found we both had it. Thus, in the face of our disbelieving, misbelieving, would-be-believing friends, we ran.

As time drew us closer to the Big Day, Kay came up with our game plan. Since we were used to talking while we ran, we'd "chat" until we reached thirteen miles. After that, she'd discuss Middle East policy. At fifteen miles, I'd take over and cover U.S. economic policy. At seventeen, we'd discuss graffiti on New York's subways; at eighteen miles, the topic was books; at twenty, the night's dinner menu. At twenty-one, we'd tell jokes.

And for the last five miles, we'd tell each other how very wonderful we were.

And oh, we felt wonderful when we boarded our flight. We had decided to fly first class, and the champagne was bubbly and the service lovely and the flight so very sophisticated—and when we arrived in Paris our hotel on the Left Bank was charming, and the city was just as magical and glittering as it ever was. We had a grand time strolling and lunching in cafés and shopping in chic Parisian boutiques. But all too soon, reality appeared in front of us in the form of Race Day.

The day of the marathon dawned cold, wet, and dreary. But how could a little rain dampen our enthusiasm? we asked. By the time we managed to find the starting line, we were destined to be at the back of the pack—although the French definition of "start," as we discovered, was somewhat loose. Instead of waiting for a flag or a whistle, everyone just started running while Kay and I stood there trying to figure out what was going on. When we finally set out, we quickly found that traffic—diesel-fueled traffic—was a part of the course, and we played tag with the darting bicycles while our feet pounded on slick, wet cobblestones.

We ran happily for thirteen miles, but at thirteen miles, only Kay cared about the Middle East. The reality of the 13.2 miles left to go had become all too clear to me. Where were the gay, young Frenchmen throwing flowers? Ah—there they were, as rain-soaked as us, and yet still applauding and shouting, *"Vive les blondes! Vive les femmes!"* Their support bolstered our spirits, but I was struggling. There were no bathrooms, so I had to go into a mechanic's garage and ask in fumbling French, "Can I please use your bathroom?" They graciously showed me to a room at the back of their garage, no larger than a broom closet and filled with tire irons and hubcaps and engine pieces, and I had to stoop to get in without banging my head. There I was, in a GARAGE, in a bathroom that had apparently been built for a midget, behind a door that barely closed, feeling numb and exhausted and wondering why I had ever wanted to run a marathon in the first place. But I was determined that I wouldn't stop now.

Finally we entered the lovely Bois de Vincennes. There we started passing big, strong men—hundreds of them, many running at a turtle's pace or walking, no less. What pride! We felt positively euphoric. The seventy-year-old couple trotting easily next to us— veterans of nineteen marathons—told us that many people start out too fast and have to finish by walking. Kay and I were still running, but as we left the woods, at twenty-one miles, I hit THE WALL.

Kay felt terrific. I hated her. She talked happily; I could barely breathe. She pointed out things to me; I could only see my feet. She told me I looked great; I couldn't stand her. My friend with the shared goal and the esprit de corps became my enemy as she kept urging me on, telling me that the finish, the Eiffel Tower, was near. But I couldn't see it, and kept asking people, "*Où est la Tour Eiffel?*" And they'd say in English, "Oh, it's just ahead!" But it never was. I figured that we must be lost, or more logically, that the Eiffel Tower had been moved or stolen. I became thoroughly convinced that someone had stolen the Eiffel Tower. This enraged me enough to go the last mile, determined to prove to all of France that their great monument had been taken and no one had noticed but me. When it finally came into view, I could barely see it through the tears and rain that were streaming down my face. We crossed the finish line to shouts of "*Vive L'America!*" because we had American flags on our shirts.

I had made it, and I didn't care. Kay had made it, and was ecstatic.

I suppose both of these reactions are typical when we finally complete a task that has taken months and months of time and commitment. The marathon was over—4 hours and 54 minutes after we'd started. It was eight P.M., cold and dark as we fought our way home on the Metro. And it was while riding beneath the incredible city whose pavement we had just pounded for 26.2 miles that our new self-esteem began to take shape. The praise from the other passengers meant little compared to our own feelings of self-achievement and accomplishment. I had done something that I wasn't at ALL sure I'd be able to do—and boy, did it feel great.

Marathons are a life-changing experience because they push you to discover the part of yourself that is a warrior. You start off and people are cheering and clapping, and there's music playing, and it's all just grand—but then there comes the part where you hit the wall and feel like you can't take another step. Somehow you keep putting one foot in front of the other, even though you're in pain

> *I had done something that I wasn't at ALL sure I'd be able to do—and boy, did it feel great.*

from the blisters on your feet, or you have a cramp in your leg, or everyone else is running past you, and no matter how tough it gets, you find it in yourself to keep going. And if you keep going, you eventually get to the end. You find out what you are really made of.

After Paris, I ran marathons for many years. I ran one in London, and one in Honolulu—where it was 104 degrees and hula dancers with hoses stood by the side of the road to spray us down—and one in Los Angeles, one in Washington, D.C., and several more in New York. And during those years, I always had those special shoes I loved: my yellow Saucony running sneakers, which I wore for almost every race. And although I went through many, many pairs—you have to get new shoes often when you're training for marathons or you'll hurt your feet—I kept buying them until Saucony discontinued the style because I liked them and because they came to represent my success. When I put those shoes on, I felt that warrior instinct kick in. . . . I knew that I was going to push through one step and then the next, and then the next, and that eventually I would triumph.

> *Aging is like a marathon.*

The very end of a marathon, when the people coming across the finish line are those who are in pain or disabled or sometimes in wheelchairs, is really quite something to see. These are people who have put themselves out for nothing. Because you don't GET anything from doing a marathon, except the knowledge that you finished something you started that is very, very hard and not fun to do. Every time I was convinced that I had to stop and give up, I was forced to dig deeper inside myself and find a wellspring of strength and fortitude that I didn't know existed. And I think that in many ways, aging is like a marathon. There's no real glory in getting to the end—we all get there one day—but the key is to stay in the race and continue putting one foot in front of the other until we cross the finish line on our own terms. Doing so brings its own reward. Even when our joints ache and our feet hurt and we'd rather be sitting at home on the couch, we need to challenge our bodies to get up and MOVE and walk out the front door. A body in motion stays in motion, and we need to keep generating that physical energy if we don't want to come to rest before our time.

When I was little, my favorite story was about Ferdinand the Bull. Ferdinand was a big, strong bull who didn't have any desire to fight the other bulls—all he wanted to do was sit under a cork tree and smell the flowers. He LOVED those flowers. And like him, for most of my life, I had no real desire to fight any bulls. Competition really didn't interest me—I liked playing tennis and skiing down lovely slopes, but the minute something felt like work I would lose interest. I didn't care about playing tennis WELL, or playing golf WELL, or mastering Jane Fonda workouts, or skiing black diamonds at all. Until the day I was introduced to running, I was quite happy being just like Ferdinand—

> *The key is to stay in the race and continue putting one foot in front of the other until we cross the finish line on our own terms.*

admiring the flowers in my living room and reading on the couch.

Perhaps this was because, at least in part, I had never been one to worry about my weight. Unlike many of the other actresses I knew, I never got upset if I gained two or three pounds. Worrying about my weight seemed like a huge waste of time, and for most of my life, I didn't even own a scale. I loved to eat and I loved food, and while I wasn't always the healthiest eater—I would just as soon have had chocolate cake and marshmallows for breakfast as anything else—I liked vegetables and fish and a lot of other good-for-you foods, so it worked out fine. As I got older, exercising and running marathons gave me a lot of leeway in this regard; the best part of all that training was being able to eat whatever I wanted—pasta, whipped cream, french fries, cheesecake—whenever I wanted it, without the slightest bit of guilt.

But when I turned fifty and began to grapple with all the parts of my life that were changing—my role on *Guiding Light*, my looks, my hormones, Renny going to Iraq, my mother's dementia, and my father's cancer—it wasn't so easy to take care of myself physically. I had always been a bundle of energy, arriving on set at seven A.M., powering through a day of taping, rushing home to run errands, exercise, shower, and then meet Steve and some friends for dinner. But now that energy seemed to be fading like the air out of a deflated balloon. The hours I spent at work, watching the younger actresses in the spotlight, left me feeling miserable and drained. My fear over what might happen to Renny consumed me. And then, of course, taking care of my parents was painful and exhausting. It was a very dark time for me, and all the feelings of diminishment and sadness began to overwhelm me.

It was around this time that the depression hit, and finally I just stopped exercising. Up until then, even though I was no longer running marathons, I had been fairly disciplined about staying in shape through walking, playing tennis, and going for the occasional jog. But now, with everything I was juggling, I felt like I truly didn't have the time. So I stopped—cold turkey. And at first it was great. I loved not having to get up early to walk through Central Park, and it certainly freed my schedule—I now had an extra two hours in my day to think about everything that was going wrong in my life. But my body was used to being active, and I didn't anticipate that the loss of those endorphins would only make my depression worse. Without exercise to keep me going and relieve some of the stress, it wasn't long before I crashed and retreated from everything, resigned to the idea that my life as I had known it was essentially over.

I became like Ferdinand the Bull once more, sitting and going nowhere, day after day—except without his happy-go-lucky attitude. Every afternoon when I arrived home from the set, I would put on sweatpants and bunny slippers and plant myself in front of the television. Instead of going out to dinner with friends, I would sit there, watching movies and eating ice cream and warm brownies. I watched *Pride and Prejudice* fifty-eight times—all eight hours, the BBC version with Colin Firth—and *Bridget Jones's Diary* eighteen times. I loved Bridget because she gave me permission to be fat, and I ate gallons and gallons of chocolate Häagen-Dazs. I would get the kind with the ribbon of fudge in the center and eat the fudge swirl right out of the carton. And I would microwave it for exactly ten seconds beforehand so the ice cream was soft and delicious and a little bit melted around the sides. I became absolutely masterful at this, because having the perfect temperature for my ice cream was the only thing in my life that I could control.

Food began to rule my life. I started to keep bagfuls of candy in my dressing room at work. And then—as if the chocolate ice cream waiting for me at home in my kitchen wasn't enough—I would stop at California Pizza Kitchen after work and order a pizza and a hot fudge sundae. Even all the time I spent caring for my parents outside the city didn't help—the food at the assisted living facility was fabulous, and I seized on this as the silver lining and indulged in cakes and puddings and pies every time I was there. The less my parents ate, the more there was for me, and eating during those visits helped me to cope.

Not surprisingly, I began to put on weight. I went from 125 pounds to 135, then 145, then 155 . . . and then I came up with an ingenious solution: I stopped weighing myself completely. If I didn't know my weight, I reasoned to myself, it didn't make any difference how heavy I was. Ignorance was bliss. But when the costume designer at work told me that I no longer fit into the small- or medium-size purple nurse's scrubs, and that they were going to have to special order me a size large, I broke down crying.

"Size large?" I wailed at the designer. "I'm going to look like a purple whale!"

"Oh Tina, don't cry, sweetie . . . it happens."

She said "It happens" like my weight gain was a mistake, as though I didn't have any choice in the matter. But I did. I knew what I was doing to myself, but I couldn't shake the feeling that it didn't matter, that I didn't matter. Renny, my parents, my figure, my career . . . it was all a losing battle. What difference did it make if I was fat?

Other people on the show noticed and tried to help me. One day when I was hiding in my dressing room, my soap opera daughter, Beth Chamberlin, knocked on the door. We were supposed to rehearse a scene in which the two of us set out to find Beth's two ex-husbands, Phillip Spaulding and his father, Alan, who for some reason were off camping together in the wilderness. I was dreading the scene because as usual, Beth was going to be in perfect shape and impeccably dressed in stylish, sexy clothes and high, high heels (never mind that we were supposed to be tramping through the woods) while I was in my size large purple scrubs and nurse's sneakers, looking like some circus bear in a blond wig that had wandered onto the set and was busily looking for doughnuts.

Beth had been worried about how I was looking and feeling these past few months, but now she had arrived with a solution in hand: Kettlebells! Kettlebells was a Russian strength-training regimen that she credited with having transformed her body, and she had already persuaded most of the other actors on *Guiding Light* to give it a try. Every time I arrived on the set, somebody would be standing around lifting a Kettlebell and asking me if I wanted to try it. "No," I would say, ashamed, annoyed that they would even ask. Beth had turned the backstage area into some sort of gym, and sure enough, everyone was starting to look just as toned and thin and fabulous as she did. I was the only holdout.

That day, Beth came through the door holding a Kettlebell just for me. She'd had it made specially; it was pink, and I was supposed to do squats and bends and all sorts of wonderful moves with this "bell," which looked more like a cannonball with a handle than something I could ring. The bell is supposed to weigh between five and seventy pounds, but Beth had made mine in a two-pound size. "Here you go, Tina!" she said gleefully, handing me the bell, which had a bright pink ribbon tied to the handle. I loved her for trying. It was adorable-looking, but I knew that the magic of Kettlebells was not going to happen for me. I wasn't ready.

At that point, exercise was the furthest thing from my mind. And while it made me sad to open the closet and see my yellow running shoes sitting there gathering dust, the thought of putting them back on was unimaginable. My body would never be the way it once was; exercise was just another part of my life that was in the past. Besides, the couch was comfortable. It was my safe place and I liked it there. I could sit and eat and forget about aging, and not have to worry about who I was or wasn't anymore. I had given up.

Steve and Renny also noticed of course—how could they not? There was so much MORE of me to notice—but they were powerless to do anything about it. I'd be reaching for the ice cream and would catch Steve watching me with a concerned expression on his face, and I'd snap, "Steve, don't look at me like that! I'm going to eat this and you can't stop me." Even if they had tried to take the food out of my hands, I honestly think I would have fought them off. Food was my anesthesia, my way of getting through the day. Steve and Renny never stopped loving me, no matter how much weight I gained, but I couldn't see myself in their eyes. Despite the size large scrubs and increasing numbers on the scale, all I felt was that I had disappeared.

Back when television was live, one of the actors I played with on *Search for Tomorrow* was killed off—his character was eaten by a bear—but he needed one more day of work to qualify for his health insurance. The next day, he snuck back into the studio during the live taping and walked onto the set, hidden by a scarf and a coat and a hat. In the middle of the scene, he tore off his disguise, looked at the camera and said, "I'm alive! I'm alive! It's a miracle!" Well, it IS a miracle to be alive, and I try to remember that all the time. (And by the way, he got his insurance.)

On any given day, I constantly need to remind myself of how lucky I am to be able to play in the arena at all, even when it feels like the opposite is true. If I'm tired or achey or my back hurts—as is often the case as we get older—I remind myself sternly, "You're not dead yet, get up!" and force my body to move and keep going.

I was in the thick of my depression and must have been close to 170 pounds when Steve and I got a call from Renny saying he was going back to Iraq. He was going be stationed at the United States Embassy in Baghdad doing counterintelligence work, and he couldn't tell us how long he'd be there—maybe as little as three months, possibly six. At the time, Baghdad was front and center in the war in Iraq, with insurgent attacks and car bombings every day, and if I'd been terrified when Renny was in Al Anbar province, I now felt a new level of fear. Renny tried to reassure me that he would be safe by telling me that he'd be working, eating, and sleeping inside the embassy.

He had barely been there for two weeks when I arrived at the CBS studios for work one morning and stopped dead in my tracks. There, on the massive television screen in the lobby, was a picture of the U.S. Embassy in Baghdad. It was being bombed. The footage showed chaos, raging fires, smoke, and debris and people running everywhere—*Oh God, Oh God*—and in that moment, I made a promise: *God, if you keep Renny safe, I swear that I'll never eat carbohydrates or sugar ever again.* I'm not sure what made those words pop into my head—but at that point in my life, it was without a doubt the absolute hardest thing I could have sworn to do.

Thankfully, we learned a few hours later that Renny was safe. And I kept my promise. I cleaned out the refrigerator and got rid of all the ice cream, and threw out the M&M'S in my dressing room at work. I started eating more salads and loading up on fruit and yogurt, and it was AGONY at first, just agony. But every time I walked by a bakery or a California Pizza Kitchen, I thought of Renny and reiterated my pledge to the Powers that be. If there was any possible way that I could help protect him and bring him home, then I would do it, no matter what it took.

It wasn't long before I realized that if I continued just sitting around the house watching television, the temptation to start eating would be too powerful to resist—so I made myself get up and go outside whenever I felt the cravings kick in, even if it was just to walk around the block. I would find a store to pop into, or bring a book to the park, or stand and watch the street performers outside the subway. I forced myself to do these things without a lot of forethought so I didn't have time to make excuses—I would simply grab my coat and go. And I found that I did feel better as a result. Being out in the world and interacting with other people, and realizing that my own two legs could still take me somewhere worthwhile pulled me out of myself and cleared my head, if only for a few minutes. I began to feel some of my old energy creeping back.

> *You learn to silence the voice that tries to cajole you with excuses and reasons why it would be better to just sit this one out.*

The food I was eating definitely helped, too—and as much as I hate to admit it, it's true what they say about having more energy if you eat less sugar and fewer carbs. All that sugar I'd been eating had made my moods go up and down, and every time they went down, I ate—which made me feel better UNTIL the next sugar crash when I would have to eat again. In hindsight, I'm sure that this exacerbated my depression. When I started eating "better," I felt cleaner and lighter. No one can tell me that steamed carrots and shredded cabbage are more fun to eat than a hot fudge sundae, because they're not. But let's face it, by that point, I wasn't really having much fun with the sundaes either.

Slowly but surely the weight came off. And by the time we got the news that Renny was headed home, I had already lost twenty pounds. It felt good, and even after he had safely returned to U.S. soil, I kept my promise because I was so grateful. But I also kept it because I realized that in a way, I had betrayed my body before it ever betrayed me. I had let the fear of what was happening to me now and what was to come as I got older terrify me into giving up the fight.

One thing I learned from running is that in every marathon, there comes a point where you hit THE WALL. You might hit it at mile twenty-one or mile twenty-five, but you almost always hit it, no matter how hard you've trained. The wall is that place where you simply run out of energy, the moment when your body wants to concede defeat and stop. So when you train, a large part of what you're conditioning yourself to do is find the mental stamina to break through the wall and keep going. You learn to silence the voice that tries to cajole you with excuses and reasons why it would be better to just sit this one out. You learn to resist the urge—no matter how powerful it may be—to just plop down on the curb and throw in the towel.

But the truth is that there are many walls in our lives that we have to face: Aging is one of them; laziness is another. A strong body can help us break through many of the walls that rise up to thwart us as we get older. But keeping ourselves strong and healthy is a daily exercise. Energy begets energy and what we put in, we get back out. We have to push ourselves to finish the race, and keep moving forward, no matter what.

My Aunt Ano walked seven miles a day until she was eighty-nine. Whenever I drove out to visit her and take her to lunch, she would bring along the Yellow Pages to help her step up into my large SUV. She steadfastly refused to let me help her, and she remained remarkably resilient and independent as a result. Contrast this with my mother, who was so pretty and delicate and would just sit in her chair and direct everyone to bring her things. Once when I was in an airport with Renny, I asked him why he never offered to carry my suitcase. And he said, "Mom, you can either be Gongee [my mother's grandmothery name] or Ano. It's your choice." He had a good point (or hmmm, then again, maybe he just didn't want to carry my suitcase).

I recently read *The Tipping Point* by Malcolm Gladwell, and in that book he talks about a phenomenon called the broken-window syndrome. The idea is that a neighborhood can be nice and clean, but if you break just one window and leave it unrepaired, you can actually watch as people start to ruin the surroundings, and eventually the whole block falls into disrepair. Well, I think that as we get older, our bodies are like that neighborhood—if we let things go and allow a broken window and stop exercising and neglect taking care of ourselves, we can end up frail and helpless before our time. When the blues hit or my joints ache, it's tempting to just lie down and take a nap. Lying on the couch feels great . . . until it becomes the only option.

When I stopped exercising and turned to food for comfort, it took a major turn of events—the bombing of the embassy and my fear for Renny's safety—to snap me out of my self-destruction. For some people, it takes a health crisis such as a heart attack to make them start to change their ways. We need to be creative and figure out SOMETHING that can make being active easier or even fun.

For my friend Trudy, that "something" was cute, toned, and way too young. Several years ago, she and I both belonged to a local gym where we would meet up before work a few mornings a week. One day she told me she had signed up for a personal trainer. I was impressed by her commitment . . . until I noticed that she was now coming to the gym at nine A.M. with her hair done and her makeup perfectly applied. When I raised an eyebrow, she assured me that she had appointments right after her one-on-one session with Mark.

Mark, the trainer, was of course adorable—and about twelve years old to boot (at least he seemed that way to us). But Trudy was looking great, and it wasn't long before I thought I might as well see what all the fuss was about. So I started training with Mark, too. One morning, after my early training session, I had the misfortune to bump into Trudy on my way out of the gym. She looked at me knowingly and said, "Tina, take off your sunglasses." I had no choice but to show her that behind my black shades I was wearing eyeliner, eye shadow, and even mascara even though it was only eight A.M.!

It wasn't really about him, we knew. It was about what he stood for: youth, possibilities, fitness (duh). I had a husband and Trudy had beaus (plural) and we both had children—quite grown—and yet here we were caring about what we looked like when working out. It wasn't just us—Mark had sent two other women we knew floating off in a haze of charm after spin class. They were dazed and giddy like teenage girls, even though they were both mothers of college kids. They offered glib denials— "Not for me, for my daughter!" HA! All of us knew why we were there. But it got us to the gym on a regular basis—and that in itself was an accomplishment.

Of course, the reality is that our bodies have changed and can no longer do what they once did, and that has to be taken into account. A few years ago, Steve and I took Renny with us on a vacation to Mexico. One day, we all decided to climb a very large Mayan ruin. Steve and I had no problem jauntily ascending the narrow stairs, but we experienced a massive jolt when we got to the top and looked down. We were so high up and the way down was sooo steep that we both just froze. Renny happily breezed along down the very steep incline while Steve and I clung to a rope, taking each step backward so we wouldn't have to see where we were going. I didn't regret going to the top of the temple and savoring the fantastic view, but oh, was I terrified as we came down.

This is a perfect example of how our age can sneak up on us, but we have to resist the urge to use our deteriorating physical abilities as an excuse to opt out. Sadly, we need to modify our activities. Sure, I can push myself to ski for six hours straight like I used to, but I'm going to have to spend two hours in the hot tub and on the massage table and stretching afterward in atonement. Maybe we can no longer play thirty-six holes of golf, but we can play eighteen or nine, and that can be just as enjoyable. That said, it's hard not to let your stubborn streak get the best of you. I once took a yoga class and forced myself to keep up with the two forty-something women who were in the group, and was thrilled when I could do everything they did—but I paid the price with a migraine that lasted for days afterward. I forgot who I was and got caught up in the moment. At our age, pushing too hard can backfire if the main goal is to feel good and be able to get out and about in the world.

These days I no longer belong to a gym, but I still do yoga about three times a week with a private teacher who works at my pace (although sometimes I still have to remind him how old I am when he starts getting overzealous with the poses). Yoga keeps me flexible, and I do it because I want to be able to get up easily from chairs, or hop in and out of cars, and it also builds core strength, which is good for my posture. I also do A LOT of walking, which suits me because it's kind to my body, and it's easy to amble just about anywhere in New York City. My friend Maria gave me a pedometer so I can count the number of steps I take each day. The medical experts say that your goal should be ten thousand steps, so if one day I only walk eight thousand (which is easy to do just going about my daily business) the next day I'll challenge myself to do twelve thousand to make up the difference. The counting and the game of it and the urge to top myself really motivate me to get up and go.

Some friends and I also have a walking group, and our rule is that you just show up in the morning at the meeting spot at the regular time. We used to call each other to coordinate, but everyone would try to move the time up or back, and it made it too easy for people to back out. Now we have a set time, do or die, and since there are several women, if one person cancels the others still have companions. Exercising with friends can be a great way to stay committed; on those days when I really don't feel like moving, the thought of seeing my friends and catching up on the latest news is ultimately what gets me out the door.

My friend Alina does something similar. She and ten of her friends all do Zumba together, which is a combination of rumba and aerobic dance. They go twice a week and take a class with this young, sexy Venezuelan instructor who makes them laugh and gets them moving. "It's fun," she told me, "and very, very aerobic. You can't believe how much we move around the room. But it's really great for me, because I love dancing. It's the Latin thing. It's in my blood."

The bottom line with exercise is that you have to, as the Nike commercial says, "Just do it." Whenever I'm tempted to wimp out and go have a cupcake, I'll chant my favorite mantra over and over: "If I did it yesterday, I can do it today." And when I make an effort to be active, I find that I really do have more energy. I feel stronger, I sleep better, and as a result I'm more likely to eat better because I don't need to reach for the nearest sugar fix to pep me up. Those endorphins can still go a long way toward keeping us young, even if we're not running marathons anymore.

Energy doesn't only come from exercise. The people we surround ourselves with can also make an enormous difference. Before I found my current walking group, I used to walk in the park with a woman who was very bright, but terribly negative. She complained about everything: her apartment, her superintendent, the construction outside, the noise next door, her daughter-in-law, her new husband, her ex-husband . . . it just went on and on. This woman was a PhD, and I'd wanted to walk with her because she was smart and I'd hoped we'd have some interesting conversations. But there was always something wrong, and I finally had to say to her, "Listen, I love walking with you, but can we stop this negativity? Let's talk about the news. Let's talk about anything besides all these little grievances. Life is too short." She got the message and she stopped.

The wonderful thing about this stage of life is that we're old enough to choose who we spend time with. At this point, I value humor and loyalty above all else. When I was younger, I felt more reluctant about distancing myself from people, but now I know that nothing saps my energy like people who are always down. I call these people Eeyores, after the donkey in *Winnie the Pooh* who is always feeling bad and depressed. Eeyores bring everyone around them down into their little pits of misery—and if there's one thing that growing older has taught me, it is that there is nothing worse than being caught up in someone ELSE'S misery. There's very little point in surrounding ourselves with negative people when the best thing we can do right now is enjoy the positives in our lives.

I'm just as strict with myself when it comes to complaining. My own personal rule about attitude is: DON'T COMPLAIN, EVER about ANYTHING. I hate complaining because it's BORING, and no one wants to be around you if you're boring. I even bore myself when I get caught up in a negative train of thought. And I do, for sure. Going on about our latest irritability, whether it's a draft we're sitting in or a hip replacement, is also the surest way to drive young people away. Brooke Astor said that we should make one new young friend a year, as they keep us current and plugged into the world—but if all we do is gripe about our old age, we'll scare them off and miss out on all that youthful energy.

When I was in my fifties, Steve and I became very good friends with Alistair Cooke, the legendary journalist and host of *Masterpiece Theatre*, and his wife, Jane. They were both in their nineties, and we used to go and visit them every Tuesday at six P.M. and have a couple of cocktails. Alistair would tell us stories that were just fabulous, and I adored Jane—she had been a painter and raised five children, and she always looked lovely and was just glorious. She and I would discuss her paintings, which were hanging all over their apartment. And she never, ever complained, which made me admire her tremendously. She had terrible arthritis in her fingers and had had to give up painting, and a few years later when Alistair died, she had to move out of the beloved apartment they'd lived in together for most of their lives. And yet she kept going—she went to movies and museums and to lunch with friends. She never stopped and she never, ever gave in. Only once, when I went out to dinner with her, did she even hint that things were difficult: She said, "This is so awful, dear. This getting old is so awful." And I almost resented her for it, because she had made me believe that it was possible to take all the hard knocks of aging in perfect stride. But except for that one time, she never complained. This was, of course, one of the reasons that I so enjoyed being around her—and I'm convinced that it is the key to keeping people close to us as we get older.

Even if we're good about keeping our fears and grievances to ourselves, we also have to fight the voice inside our heads that tells us it's easier to just give up the fight. I still get the blahs from time to time, when I'll start to think, "Oh, I'm too tired to cook dinner/put myself together/get my roots colored/exercise/buy a special present for my niece." We all feel this way occasionally, but I'll make myself go for a walk, or go visit a friend, or even go to a movie by myself (this is one of my favorite things to do, and I do it a lot—I'll buy popcorn and sit on the aisle and watch the movie, and when it's over I feel very empowered for having ventured out on my own). By pushing to get out, to change the scenery, I am able to resist the feelings of sadness.

There is also a lot to be said for making your bed and doing the dishes; placing some fresh flowers around helps, too. My niece, whenever she's feeling drab and wallowing, will invite people over since it makes her clean up the house and get in the shower and blow-dry her hair. These little victories can be so gratifying, and give us the energy we need to keep going.

One Christmas, I was in a bit of a funk, and I just didn't feel like doing the whole "big show." Normally, our apartment looks like a scene from *The Nutcracker* with a huge tree and presents galore, and all sorts of decorations that I've bought over the years; I start the carols on December 1 and play them nonstop until the New Year. But that year, I just didn't feel like going to all the trouble to put things up. I started thinking, "What's the point?" But I pushed myself to do it and the reward was huge: Whenever I walked into the apartment, I was instantly cheered to hear the carols and see the tree all lit up. And it gave me an excuse to invite people over—I had a constant stream of friends stopping by, which perked me up even more. Sometimes when we're in a rut, we need to force ourselves to act like the person we want to be . . . and then the reality almost always follows.

It's easy in this phase of life to focus on what we're missing or what's changed, but most of us still have a lot to be thankful for.

My friend Jean told me that her husband, David, used to turn to her at the end of every party and say, "Aren't we lucky?" She told me this after David had died. So now, whenever I feel myself getting down or focusing on the gaps in my life, I say to myself, "Aren't I lucky?" and force myself to think of at least five things I'm grateful for. I felt like a Pollyanna the first few times I tried it, but it does work.

As we get older, we need to always remember that we are lucky . . .

To take walks in the park
To be able to exercise
To eat good food
To go places with friends
To see new things
To laugh
To have family
To have faith in our own wisdom and strength
To be able to change our shoes whenever we want

Sometimes when I'm out walking in Central Park, I still get seized by the impulse to run, especially when I'm near the Reservoir. Sometimes I even imagine that I'm wearing my bright yellow Sauconys. The memories come flickering back: the pink bloom of the cherry trees in spring, the ice on the water in winter, the friends I've run around and around the track with, and the exhilaration of waking up early and throwing on my sneakers, going outside and running fifteen miles. But I have to remind myself that walking is what's best for me now, and that there's so much to enjoy with every step I take. I look down and see my sensible but still brightly colored yoga shoes, and I breathe in and out, and feel my heart pumping, and smile at the joggers and people on bikes. I love knowing that my feet can still carry me places. When I am very old and very worn out, I hope that one of my last acts will be walking around the Reservoir, putting one foot in front of the other, savoring the beauty all around me, and preparing to face another mile.

Listen to Your Heart, Not Your Stomach

When I was younger, I tried a few crazy diets just because my friends were doing them, too: the grapefruit diet, the cabbage soup diet, and some ridiculous diet whose name I can't remember where we just drank chocolate shakes for thirty days. But until I reached my fifties, I never made a serious attempt to lose weight. And when I did, I found that in addition to changing what I ate, understanding WHY I had gained the weight in the first place and trying to heal those wounds were just as important.

I believe that many women, including me, eat to drown out the pain of something that is happening to us—instead of turning to alcohol or drugs, we turn to food. When I was in my depression, I can clearly remember thinking, "The only thing that makes me feel good is this ice cream." But I believe that the pain we feel is actually our inner voice telling us that some part of our lives needs fixing. Too many of us try to eat that voice down to keep it quiet—often that's easier than facing the truth. But I think that when we feel the urge to eat, we need to stop and NOT tamp that voice down with food, but LISTEN and try to understand what it's trying to say. For me, this meant facing my fears about aging. Only then could I start making changes in my life to ease the process, and when I made those changes, I could finally let go of the food.

These days I am still not a perfect eater, and although I do stick to my no-carbs-no-sugar rule most of the time, I still get a hankering for sweets and Starbucks' Mocha Frappuccinos (I always tell myself that it's just coffee). For me, sugar is like a former lover that I don't think I'll ever be over entirely. I'll pass by a bakery and think, "Oh dear God, do I want that pumpkin pie." But I recognize that being healthy is an ongoing process, and that every day is an opportunity to make good choices.

There are a million books and diet gurus who will tell you what you should and should not do to lose weight. But my advice is to just be NORMAL. To me, normal means getting some exercise, eating fairly healthy, and allowing yourself the occasional indulgence because food is there to be enjoyed and there's nothing wrong with that. Normal means NOT thinking about food—either how to eat it or how to avoid it—for the majority of the day. And most of all, normal means living a life that fulfills all the various aspects of your being *OTHER* than your stomach. Listen to that voice inside you when it starts to speak, because it will tell you what you really need . . . and most of the time, it's not chocolate.

CHAPTER EIGHT

Climb Every Mountain

One evening, Steve and I were out to dinner with two of our close friends, Penni and Petr. Penni was telling us that she had just joined the board of Outward Bound, the well-known, nonprofit organization dedicated to helping people explore the world and expand themselves and their potential through wilderness trekking and travel. She was thrilled with her news, and said that to celebrate, she was in the process of planning a trip to Africa with the rest of the board to climb Mount Kilimanjaro.

"Oh, Tina, why don't you come along?" she asked brightly. "There's a whole group of us going, and you'll get to travel and do some real mountain climbing. It's just the sort of challenge you love."

She was obviously remembering my marathon days and assuming that I was in far better shape than I was. But in a moment of bravado, assisted by a few too many glasses of sauvignon blanc, I heard myself say, "Yes, I'd love to."

I immediately regretted my decision. *Why did you say yes?* I chastised myself as Steve and I walked home that night. *What were you thinking? Mount Kilimanjaro?* I wasn't even sure where Mount Kilimanjaro was. A quick look in the encyclopedia when I got home told me that it stands 19,341 feet above the plains of Tanzania—about 19,000 feet too high for me. *I'll call Penny tomorrow and tell her I can't go,* I comforted myself as I crawled into bed that night.

I always read before going to sleep, and that night I happened to be reading a book Steve had gotten me called *Genghis Khan and the Making of the Modern World* by Jack Weatherford. I loved the book. Genghis Khan's life fascinated me, and as I lay there reading about his spirit quests—the journeys he would take into the mountains before a big battle to find himself and his inspiration—there was one passage in particular that struck a chord in me: "The genius of Genghis Khan did not come from epiphanies or sudden flashes of insight, but from a persistent willingness to try new things. In every battle he fought, Genghis tried something new. He never fought the same war twice." That passage really affected me—it had been so long since I tried anything new.

That night, I had a dream. I dreamed that I was climbing a mountain and it was dark. I couldn't see and I was cold and alone. In the dream, I knew that I should be frightened, but I wasn't. Alone on the mountain, I actually felt peaceful for the first time in years.

The next morning, I decided not to call Penny and cancel. Kilimanjaro was going to be my spirit quest. I'd never climbed a mountain before and now was as good a time as any to give it a try. Besides, I reassured myself: I'd be traveling with a bunch of nonprofit board members from Manhattan. How hard could it be?

In the weeks that followed, I made preparations. I bought all sorts of exciting gear including a bright pink parka with matching pink snow boots (how could I resist?), a huge backpack, and a pink sleeping bag that the rugged young guy at the North Face store (who had to order it for me, since for some reason they didn't have pink in stock) guaranteed would keep me warm in temperatures as low as forty degrees below zero. I visited my doctor and received the obligatory vaccinations for yellow fever, typhoid, and a host of other lovely diseases. "You know what you're getting into, I presume," my doctor said sternly when I told him about the trip. "It's a spirit quest," I said happily. He didn't get it. Steve and Renny watched all of my frantic preparations with amazement—but they never uttered a word of discouragement.

Before long, I'd assembled everything I needed—a passport, visas, hair dryer, a camera, a full makeup kit, rollers for my hair, a pair of heels, and a supersize jar of peanut butter in case I got hungry—and then suddenly the trip was upon me. The night before I was scheduled to leave, the phone rang. It was Penny. She was crying and she told me tearfully that she wasn't going to be able to go. Her chronic back problem had returned, and her doctor had told her that under no circumstances was she to be hiking up any mountains. If I was going to Kilimanjaro, I was now going on my own.

I was in shock. I debated calling the whole thing off—but the sight of my backpack sitting by the front door, ready and waiting, seemed to be urging me to be brave and just go anyway. So the next morning, summoning all my courage, I boarded a plane bound for Nairobi, Kenya. From there a charter flight took me to the town of Moshi at the base of Kilimanjaro.

The day we set out, I arrived at the foot of the mountain for what I hoped would be a leisurely climb and found myself among a group of very experienced hikers. They were all wearing earth tones and eating trail mix; I was wearing neon pink from head to toe and eating my peanut butter out of the jar with my fingers (I'd been in Africa less than a day and I was already ravenous). I had my hair curled and my makeup on—after all, this was my great adventure, and the mountain looked beautiful, shouldn't I look the same? The other hikers smirked and tried to avoid me.

We had been told that our backpacks could weigh a maximum of seventy pounds. It had never really occurred to me that anyone would actually check this, so naturally I had brought along lots and lots of extra stuff. As we stood there preparing to depart, our trip leader—a tall, handsome man who looked like a cross between Harrison Ford and Brad Pitt—stepped forward and shouted, "Jambo, Bibi Bwana!" He then continued in a lightly accented, baritone voice, "This will be the most exciting trip of your lives. You will be tested like you have never been tested before. Some of you will make it to the top of the mountain, and some of you will not." He was so good-looking that I was momentarily distracted from what he was saying—and then it hit me. I tapped one of the hikers next to me. "Wait, we're climbing to the top? The very tippy top where the snow is?" He looked at me with disdain and said, "Of course." "Dear God!" I said. "I don't belong here."

It was too late.

Things got even worse when our handsome leader announced that in keeping with Outward Bound tradition, we would all be carrying our packs ON OUR BACKS. At this pronouncement I literally laughed. Everyone turned and looked at me. "Is he joking?" I pleadingly asked one of the female hikers, who just stared at me witheringly and turned her back. I looked around at the other trip members who were gamely hoisting their backpacks, and burst into tears. I could barely lift my bag off the ground much less onto my shoulders. Fortunately, one of the local porters came to my aid. He took me to a tent where I unloaded my hair dryer and curlers and makeup, and then he took some of my heaviest things and secretly put them in his bag. I was grateful to him and a little ashamed at the same time.

I wept for the first four days of the climb. The route we were taking went up the north side of the mountain rather than the more heavily trafficked south side; Outward Bound preferred to use this path as it was isolated and there were no other hikers. We slept in caves with bats—well, everyone else slept, I never closed my eyes. The first day was swelteringly hot as we trekked through the lush, tropical forests at the base of the mountain. I was carrying my lightened backpack with my sleeping bag and air mattress on top, and with every exhausting step I wondered what on earth I had been thinking. I was a soap opera actress, not a mountain climber.

What was I doing here?

When I was in college, the first play I ever appeared in was a delightful musical called *The Fine Art of Falling*. It had been written by two of my classmates, both extremely witty, and was going to be our senior class production. Boys from Yale were even going to be in it! There was an audition notice posted in the dining hall, and it read, "We are looking to cast the following parts: Lead—young, pretty girl (should be able to sing)." I stopped reading there because I couldn't sing a note, but I did check the time and place for the auditions: eight P.M. that evening, in the auditorium.

That night over dinner, I discussed it with my friends. Did I dare audition? I wanted so badly to be in that play! I had already begun thinking about acting as a career—it seemed a natural choice given my personality—but I had yet to actually DO any, save for my performance as a talking tomato in grammar school. I finally decided that just to audition would be a huge step for me, so at eight o'clock I walked over to the auditorium and sat outside the door, listening.

After three or four girls had gone in and come out, I got up the nerve to go inside. The two writers handed me the script. I read the lines and waited for a reaction. They were stunned. They loved me! Now I was stunned. Then they asked me to sing. Ahhh . . . There was silence when I told them I couldn't carry a tune. And when they heard me sing, they knew that I was right: My voice was terrible. The writers looked at each other, unsure of what to do.

They asked me to have a seat while they did the rest of the auditions. Another girl came in, and boy, could she sing, but she wasn't as right for the part as I was. They kept trying to see if I could belt the songs or something. Finally they gave me the part, and decided that I would speak/sing the easy songs, and the other girl would sing the hard songs *about* me like a sort of narrator or Greek chorus. I was elated!

The play itself was about skiing. My character meets a boy on the ski slopes and hops on the chairlift with him, completely forgetting that she can't ski. When they arrive at the top, she tries to follow him down the slalom—and ends up falling all the way down and crashing and breaking her leg. It was about falling down ski slopes, but more important, falling in love—and the songs we sang were just adorable: "All alone on a chairlift with you, I'm so glad that there's room for just two, will I do as the someone who shows you the view?" Or my favorite:

The fine art of falling is easily learned
By even the hardest of hearts;
You wake up one morning, the tables they have turned,
The horse back in front of the cart.

I still have those songs on an old record, and the fact that I sang as many as I did is appalling, but oh, how I loved being in that play. We did a total of five performances and brought the house down every night.

In the years that followed, I often thought back to the name of the play: *The Fine Art of Falling.* I loved that phrase, because for me it really captured something I believed in—the art of taking risks. The risk my character in the play had taken for love, and the risk that I had taken by daring to audition in the first place were both perfect examples of taking a leap of faith and hurtling yourself into the unknown . . . and ultimately coming out okay.

That play served as a kind of blueprint for me, and I continued to take risks throughout my life: I defied my mother's wishes and pursued acting, I kept pursuing it even when no one would take my calls, I kept trying to have a baby even when the odds were against me, and I jumped at the chance to do things like climb Kilimanjaro even when rational thought suggested I do otherwise. And whenever I wondered if I was brave enough to take another chance, or stretch beyond my

> *Whenever I wondered if I was brave enough to take another chance, or stretch beyond my normal range, or try something completely new . . .*

normal range, or try something completely new—or when it seemed like I might have finally bitten off too much, as it did when I was struggling up that mountain—I reminded myself that I was an EXPERT at the Fine Art of Falling, and that most of the time, with perseverance, I landed on my feet.

I think it is our natural tendency as we get older to stop taking risks and choose the more familiar path. Failure looks a lot more frightening at our age. It is so much easier to daydream about the things we'd like do: write a novel, go skiing in the Canadian Bugaboos, or start playing guitar. But for me, the single easiest way to feel youthful again is to break out of my normal routine and try something unexpected. I don't want to live out the last years of my life doing the same things and seeing the same faces (as much as I love them) every single day. I want to keep learning and growing and having new observations about life. Even my mother, who so often played it safe, said to me in her later years, "Tina, the only things I regret in my life are the ones I didn't do." I may be approaching seventy, but I refuse to believe that adventure is something that has passed me by.

. . . I reminded myself that I was an EXPERT at the Fine Art of Falling, and that most of the time, with perseverance, I landed on my feet.

I read an article years ago about a man who was a famous parachute jumper. For years, he had been known for jumping out of planes and performing all these tricks on the way down. Then one day, he jumped and his parachute didn't open. But he still did the whole performance, the whole spectacle, there in midair as he plummeted to his death. And that for me says everything. He knew he was going to die, and still he gave everything he had to those last moments and did something worthy of remembrance.

My friend Jean's husband, David, was Harvard class of '55—and he particularly enjoyed spending time with the Radcliffe graduates at the reunions. Like many women of their generation, the "Cliffies" had received a top-tier education, but were essentially educated to marry well. But from about the twenty-fifth reunion on, their children were grown, so many of them were starting their careers in their fifties. "He found this fascinating," Jean recalled. "David always wanted somebody to do a book about that class. Just as their husbands were slowing down, these women were starting companies or trying new professions and completely redefining themselves. And the higher the number of the reunion, the more interesting their lives became. It was very inspiring."

> *It's easy to reach this stage in life and feel like we've done it all.*

It's easy to reach this stage in life and feel like we've done it all, or that the best is behind us. But we can't fall into the trap of only thinking about the past, or talking about the past—we need a present, too. When I meet new people today, most of them don't care that I was on a soap opera, or even if they do, I'm not going to be the one to bring it up. We need to have interesting things that we're doing RIGHT NOW so that we can be interesting both to ourselves and to others.

For me, travel is one of my favorite ways to have adventures on a regular basis. Every winter, my friend Anne and I take a trip

to some new foreign destination—the more foreign the better—
and I find that nothing wakes me up like being in a place where I
don't speak the language and have to be really on my game. So far
we've been to Hong Kong, India, Turkey, Thailand, Vietnam,
Cambodia, and Dubai. For friends who
know me, this is somewhat incredible,
as I hate, hate, HATE to fly. Once
when I was younger, I was seated next
to a woman on a plane who turned to
me as we were taking off and said,
"Just think: One hundred thousand
moving parts, all made by the lowest
bidder." Well, that was it for me—I've
never been able to get that image out
of my head, so it takes some major

> *But we can't fall into the trap of only talking about the past—we need a present, too.*

willpower (and often a sleeping pill) to get me on a plane. Since
Anne hates flying even more than I do, our trips are lessons in either bravery or insanity.

When Renny was younger, I used to insist that Steve and I
travel on separate planes so that if one of them crashed, Renny
wouldn't be left alone. One time, the two of us were flying to
Moscow and Steve had decided that we should take the same
flight because he was tired of traveling alone. I reluctantly agreed,
and there we were, thirty-five thousand feet over the Atlantic
Ocean, when the plane started bouncing around wildly. This
wasn't just normal turbulence—I could feel the plane dropping
and then pulling back up and I was convinced that we were going
into the Atlantic at any moment. As I sat there clutching the arm-
rests, nearly fainting from fear, all I could think about was Renny,
and what would happen to him if Steve and I both went plunging
into the dark, cold water below.

Finally I saw the stewardesses start the dinner service. The plane was still bouncing and pitching around, and we were supposed to be in our seats, but I was so out of my mind that I got up and tottered over to them and said, "Please, you've got to let me help you serve this meal." They looked at me, stunned, and said, "Well, we're not supposed to let you—" and I begged, "Listen, you've got to let me help or I'm going to go crazy."

I think they were so taken aback that they agreed, and for the next hour, I went up and down the aisles passing out the trays and filling glasses with wine, and picking up the trays and filling more glasses with more wine. There was a group of Russian astronauts up in front who had been in the States for some celebration with NASA, and they were drinking madly and carrying on, laughing their heads off—having been to outer space, this bit of a rattling was nothing to them. But having something to do helped me a lot (it also helped that I got away from Steve, since I was utterly furious with him for almost making Renny an orphan). By the time dinner was over, the plane had stopped shaking so I went back to my seat—and when we arrived in Moscow, the flight crew gave me a jeroboam of Bordeaux in appreciation (obviously taken from first class). One of them even asked me which routes I worked— she thought I was a real stewardess who had been off duty and just happened to be on the flight.

Even now, when Renny is in his thirties, I still think of him when the turbulence starts. But I believe that every time we give in to fear, we're losing something, so I MAKE myself fly—because I know that what awaits me on the other end is so, so worth it. For me, travel is about defying the impulse to close myself down and remain where everything is well-known and comfortable. It's about doing something that will hopefully change me in some way, or give me a new insight or a different perspective on my life.

Several years ago, Steve and I went on vacation to the tiny island of Lanai in Hawaii. We had a wonderful time enjoying the
beaches and sunshine, and the resort had everything you could
possibly want: thickly cushioned blue chaises, a maze of reflecting
pools, splendid rooms, a gorgeous golf course for Steve, and fabulous food and wines and entertainment. At the end of the week,
we made our way down to the dock to wait for the boat that
would take us back to the larger island of Maui. And as we stood
there in the fading afternoon, a glorious young man—tanned and
barefoot with sun-streaked hair wearing nothing but a tattered
pair of khaki shorts—jumped aboard a tiny sailboat and immediately turned up Beethoven on his radio. We overheard some of his
friends asking when he'd return, and he shrugged and yelled over
the haunting music, "I'm off to Molokai. I'll probably be there
for breakfast."

The youth, the freedom of that boy, the strains of music, and
the late afternoon light all conspired to sweep me away. I was
filled with longing. Tears washed down my face. To the others
around me, it looked like I hated to leave this perfectly groomed
paradise. But inside I felt the call of the wild: I wanted nothing
more than to clamber aboard my own small boat and cast off into
uncharted waters, to sail under the sky and stars throughout the
night, totally alone with nothing but the sea, and arrive on
Molokai in time for breakfast.

To this day, I hold deeply in my heart that run-down old
boat, that gorgeous boy, his bare feet, and his insouciance in the
face of the whole wide ocean as the summation of the unclut-
tered, unfettered, perfectly free life. This boy had no need for blue
chaises with drinks being served; he only needed a boat and the
abundance of the sea. I yearned to be him, and was reminded of
how little I need to make a truly happy life. This insight never

would have happened at home, and I often think back to that mystical moment whenever I find myself getting caught up in daily minutiae and worrying about the little things.

Of course there are many "little things" and hassles that we have to face when traveling as we get older. I take my sensitive stomach and my fussy nose with me wherever I go, but I force myself to handle these things and work around them, because there are always a million excuses I can make for why I CAN'T do something. And I find that I can usually have a marvelous time in spite of having "myself" there—myself that is tired from the time change, or grumpy from the crazy cab drivers, or feeling bloated from eating strange cuisines. These issues don't compare to the wonder of walking the streets where Gandhi walked, or the thrill of seeing the sunrise over the mountains of Cappadocia. As long as I have shoes to carry me places, I'm going to keep climbing aboard cars and trains and planes, and continue to get out and explore the world.

Travel is far from the only way to expand our horizons as we age. My friend Nan, who is older than I, recently decided to take up ice-skating. She lives in my neighborhood, and one morning as I went out, I happened to see her walking down the street, impeccably dressed as always but with a pair of ice skates over her shoulder. Curious, I caught up to her and asked where she was going.

"I'm heading over to Central Park to the ice rink," she told me. "I'm finally going to learn how to ice-skate."

When I mentioned the crowds of people and the possibility that she might hurt herself by slipping on the ice, she just laughed. "Sure, those things have crossed my mind," she said. "But that's no reason not to do it."

My Aunt Ano, who lived to be eighty-nine, told me that one of the scariest things she ever did was to walk into a bridge club in her local town community center and join it. She was terrified of being the outsider, but that bridge club ultimately gave her years of pleasure, and all the club members turned up at her funeral and couldn't stop talking about how wonderful she was. This story and Nan's are absolute proof that you don't have to do anything exotic or even leave town to have a new experience that broadens your world. There are dozens of little opportunities to take a risk every day.

One thing that I force myself to do on a regular basis is invite people over and have dinner parties. For some people, dinner parties are second nature, but they always cause me a lot of anxiety, partly because they're so much work: You have to invite the people, plan the menu, do the shopping, set the table, and the list goes on. Steve would be perfectly happy to just invite a handful of close friends over for beef stew and bread and some bottles of wine, but if I'm going to go to all the trouble to host, I feel like I want to go all out. I'll spend days figuring out the menu, and I'll try to come up with a theme—I once threw a dinner party on Valentine's Day where everyone came dressed as famous lovers from history (such as Romeo or Juliet) and had to figure out who their date was by a clue. But no matter how much planning I've done, when the big night arrives, I always worry that the guests won't mix, or the party won't gel, or that everyone will be bored. And to my mind, there's nothing worse than a deadly dull dinner party.

On *Guiding Light*, the dinner parties were anything but dull,

> *There are dozens of little opportunities to take a risk every day.*

and perhaps this is part of the reason I always feel such pressure. On the show, hosting a dinner party was a recipe for DRAMA. Everyone had secrets that inevitably came out during the meal and caused all sorts of repercussions, especially on Thanksgiving. One year we were all gathered in the Spaulding dining room when a ghost appeared to haunt Alan Spaulding. He had killed yet another person (he must have killed at least twenty or thirty over the course of the show), and he would jump up and be startled when this face appeared in the window and we all went on gobbling turkey and sweet potatoes as though nothing whatsoever was odd. Sometimes a policeman (Frank Cooper) would arrive and take one of the diners to jail; and sometimes someone would have a heart attack and I would have to stop shoveling food into my mouth to tend to that person. Sometimes a former husband we'd all presumed dead would walk in and disturb the meal, or a child we believed was gone forever would emerge fifteen years older than when he had left a year before. Dinners at the Spaulding mansion were very different from, say, dinners at the Coopers. With the Spauldings, expensive silver and flowers and a bit of stiffness prevailed; with the Coopers, who were a huge Greek family, chaos often ensued—people would be in the diner, eating and hugging and holding babies and using paper plates, and usually the stove broke.

Thus every time I plan a dinner party, it's impossible for me to NOT fear that some ridiculous drama will unfold—that I'll seat someone next to their archrival by mistake, or that someone will realize her husband's having an affair, or the kitchen will catch on fire, or that everyone (God forbid) will come down with food poisoning after they get home. It's a lot of responsibility bringing a large group of people together and mixing them up under one roof. I usually spend the first two hours of the party in a state of anxious apprehension . . . until I breathe a sigh of relief halfway through the meal when I look around and realize that everyone's having a good time.

I also make a point of doing things on my own, things that I would normally do with another person. Steve and I have a house in Florida, and when we first started going there, I bought a pale green, fat-tired bike so that I could ride around town. I'll go off by myself while Steve is playing golf, and find my way into different neighborhoods, or stop at some new café for lunch, and it feels exciting and brave to be doing these things on my own. When I'm home in New York, I'll go to lunch or dinner alone if Steve is working and my friends are busy, and bring a book to keep me company. I'll try the sandwich place down the street that just opened up, or whatever new restaurant all the magazines are raving about. Many of my friends say that they are embarrassed to go places alone, because they imagine that everybody else is looking at them and thinking, "Oh how sad, they don't have any friends." They won't even go to parties if they don't have someone to walk in with. But I REALLY don't think that other people are thinking about us at all—and if they are, so what? Being alone refreshes me, and a book is often the best company I can have, as I can shut it up by closing it (something you definitely cannot do with a friend or husband). Learning to be comfortable doing things on our own is extremely important as we get older— otherwise it's far too easy to sit in the house waiting for someone or something exciting to knock on your door.

Sometimes taking a risk can be as simple as seizing an opportunity—even a small one—that you would normally let pass you by. My friend Duane had been going to the same neighborhood nail salon for years when she decided to take a chance and befriend one of the other customers. "That nail salon is like a sorority house," Duane said, laughing. "It's always full of young women in their twenties and thirties, talking about who they're dating, and who's sleeping with whom, and you wouldn't believe the drama—I mean, the stories I could tell from the nail salon! I'd just sit there with my book, rolling my eyes. But over time, I kept noticing this one woman—she was my age, the unassuming type, and even though she was holding it back, I could see that she was laughing at the same things I was.

"So I finally said to my manicurist, 'What's that woman's name?' And I went over to her and said, 'I think we should have lunch because we definitely have the same sense of humor.' And now we are great friends. But that's something I never would have done when I was younger. I would have been too busy to make the effort, or I would have felt self-conscious about it. But now I just thought, 'What do I have to lose?'"

My friend Denise did something similar when, after holding back for years, she jumped at the chance to buy a little cottage in a vacation spot that she loved. She and her husband had been going to this same town for years, and they had a lot of friends in the area. They had even discussed buying on several occasions but always concluded that the time wasn't right. "But I was down there for a weekend and happened to see this house," Denise told me, "and it was just the right size, the perfect location, everything. And I just thought, 'If not now, when?' So I put in an offer without even telling Bill." Her husband was furious when he found out, but Denise knew they had the money, and sure enough—now her husband loves it. There's a garden for him to work in, and a garage where he can tinker around with his cars, and having their own house there gives them no end of pleasure. "We could have gone on thinking about it for years," Denise said. "But this is the time in our lives to enjoy it.

Every so often it's good to throw caution to the wind and act first and think later."

I believe that "What do I have to lose?" and "If not now, when?" are the very best attitudes we can have at this point in our lives. I was at a party for the Daytime Emmys several years ago when I spotted Buzz Aldrin across the room. I was standing and chatting with a group of actors who were all talking about the shows they were on, and I looked up and thought, "Dear God, that's Buzz Aldrin, the man who walked on the moon!"

I decided right then that I would go talk to him, and I summoned up my courage and made my way over to his group. He was just lovely and told me all about his experiences—and while we were standing there, my soap opera grandson, Zack Conroy, who played James Spaulding, came up to me and said, "I knew you'd be talking to the most interesting person in the room." And I loved that. I mean, here I could have been standing around talking to all these other people about who looked pretty (or not), and who'd had the latest nip and tuck, but instead I was talking to Buzz Aldrin ABOUT THE MOON!!! Although the truth was that anyone else could have talked to him, too—I just made a point of actually doing it.

And I think this goes for our work and our pastimes, too. Now is the time to stop hiding our passions and keeping them to ourselves. My friend Paula had always enjoyed photography, but when her husband was alive, most of the picture-taking fell to him. "Ray was great at producing all sorts of art," she recalls, "including photographs. So that was his domain. But in the last few years I've come back to photography. And that's one of the nice things about this phase—sometimes you pick up things that you always liked to do, but that were always done so much better by someone else, maybe your spouse. But now you feel like you have a license to try it again. So I've been doing a little photography of my own—I even put myself in an amateur show, which was fun."

My friend Crystal Chappell, who played Olivia Spencer on *Guiding Light*, did something very gutsy in her professional life after we learned the show was ending. She had been a part of the famous "Otalia" story line, in which her character Olivia and Natalia Rivera (played by Jessica Leccia) fell in love. This was one of the first lesbian romances on daytime television and it had earned us an entirely new fan base. When *Guiding Light* was over, Crystal decided that the timing was right for her to do something else for that market—so she created an online Web series called *Venice: The Series* that had a lesbian character in the lead role. She got her best friend, Kimmy, to write it, and she played the lead of Gina, a gay designer living in Venice, California. They had no idea if it would take off, but her fans flocked to it and the word spread, and the series is now very successful. The risk for her was huge, as the concept was not mainstream, but it has worked and the show is beautiful.

The ways in which we continue to grow as we get older can be as simple as taking a class at a local university—my friend Alina takes a class in contemporary art once a week that visits galleries all over town—or as grand as devoting ourselves to a cause we believe in and trying to really make a difference. My friend Jean knew a woman, Mary Ann, who up until a year before she died, was visiting refugee camps in Thailand and Afghanistan. She was in her seventies, yet she continued to travel to these very poor, very troubled parts of the world and raise money through non-profits to help those who were suffering. "She's the person I look to most when I think about the years ahead," Jean told me. "She was quite remarkable, and it just goes to show that you can still have an impact as you get older."

For me, doing my play *Changing Shoes* has allowed me to expand my range and try something completely new—but it's also enabled me to reach out to all the other women out there who fear that aging is all about wrinkles and nothing more. When the lights go down in the theater, I'm not standing backstage worrying about saying my lines perfectly, or what kind of press I'm going to get. I'm thinking, "Please let someone in the audience have an insight tonight." Because that's why I do it, even though it's terrifying. Being on that stage all alone is like being naked. And there is always a moment before every performance when I think, "What am I doing this for? Why did I take this on?" But then I remember that it's because I want people to know that they're not alone in these experiences. I felt alone for a long time and if I can inspire someone to approach life differently, to start seeing the possibilities again, then I've done my job.

I think this idea of raw possibility is what we need to hold on to as we get older. Our lives can be filled with whatever we want: romance, work, friendship, adventure—we just have to be brave enough to look for it. And have the right pair of shoes.

We reached the third and final base camp on Kilimanjaro at seventeen thousand feet after four days of relentless climbing. The camp sits exposed on a lonely outcrop of glacier and volcanic rock and when we finally arrived there, I was certain that I would never make it home. The last forty-eight hours had been brutal. High winds and freezing temperatures made for near-impossible trekking, and we were all struggling with altitude sickness, even the seasoned hikers. I had a constant, searing headache and we'd lost one of our group's leaders when she developed pulmonary edema and had to be taken down the mountain. Roughly ten climbers die on Kilimanjaro each year attempting the summit, and as I huddled in my sleeping bag listening to the roar of the wind it occurred to me without any particular fanfare that I could be one of this year's statistics.

It was then, in that moment, that I rediscovered just how much I wanted to live. I had been hiding away from the world these past ten years, gaining weight and giving up, and now here I was in a place that looked like some lunar wasteland, covered in dirt, and all I knew was that I wanted to get home alive so I could start living my life again. I decided then that I was going to make it through this trip alive, no matter what.

At midnight we started the final leg of the climb so that we could reach the summit at sunrise. It was pitch-black and I couldn't see the ground in front of me. With every step, the wind and snow intensified, and the scree—a blinding mixture of ice, snow, and gravel—swirled around me and pulled me to my knees. I crawled forward, fighting my way across a crevasse so that I wouldn't lose sight of the other climbers. But when I looked up, there was only darkness and the howling wind. The other hikers with their little headlamps had vanished. I was alone. It was just like my dream, I thought, except this time I was terrified beyond all imagining.

Where is everybody?

I collapsed onto the frozen snow. I wanted to cry, but I didn't have any tears left. I wanted to scream and curse my fate. With every second that I lay there, it grew colder and colder and the wind blew harder and I thought regretfully, *This is the end. I am going to die on a mountain in Africa.* But then—*oh thank God!* There was someone reaching out to me, a figure extending a hand out of the blackness. I looked up and saw the other climbers.

There was Lillian Raines in her nurse's uniform, still looking fabulous, and Aga smiling and smoking French cigarettes. There was Steve, holding a dozen roses and a carton of Häagen-Dazs, and Renny, saluting me: *Keep going, Mom.* My mother in her little red beret calling my name, and my father reading his newspaper, waiting for me to join him for lunch. And my friends, my wonderful friends. They were all smiling and waving me on. And then, dear God, I saw Genghis Khan. He'd come to help me. For a moment I was convinced that I had either died or lost my mind. I wiped my eyes and looked again, but there he was. He held out his hands to pull me up. And I got up, and I kept going.

And just before dawn—I reached the summit. I made it to the top.

Standing at nineteen thousand feet, I watched the sun rise up over the mountaintop and felt the light's hint of warmth on my face. I was cold and hungry and tired to the bone, but for the first time in years, just as my dream had predicted, I felt totally at peace. And then, as I stood there breathing the cold, thin air, I watched as the sun turned the glaciers and the snow on the top of the mountain bright pink. Everything was bathed in a pink neon glow. I looked down at my snow boots and smiled.

The mountain was dressing up.

Just like me.

Finding Your Own Mountains: How to Get Out the Door

On *Guiding Light*, finding adventure was amazingly easy. We must have had a fleet of Concordes at the Springfield airport, since we could arrive in Bangladesh or on an island in Bali in just three hours flat. What's more, we always landed in perfectly pressed linen clothes without a hair out of place and with no jet lag, carrying a single tiny suitcase that contained nothing but lingerie. In reality, adventure takes planning and preparation, and this alone can be a deterrent.

These days, there's no denying that the twenty-year-old on his way to Molokai has a huge advantage over us. He has no lower back pain or tummy troubles or fears of the unknown. We do. But I have tried to develop a system that makes things easy, whether I'm spending a weekend at a friend's house or taking a longer trip. I always think I'll be a different person when I arrive someplace new—one who doesn't mind a hard pillow or the coldness of the temperature—but I'm still me, no matter where the plane lands. At our age, it is NOT high-maintenance to be realistic about what we need and plan accordingly.

• *Pack Lightly.* I limit myself to two suitcases, both on wheels, so that I don't need help getting around. I don't pack more than I can reasonably carry on my own because there may not always be people to assist me (and besides, I get a kick out of knowing that I can still be self-sufficient). I edit, edit, edit what I think I will need: one sweater, five shirts, two slacks, two nighties, and five pairs of underwear and socks/stockings is a good rule, along with a pair of dress pants, a dressier sweater, and two or three dressy tops—who knows when a Maharani will ask one to dinner? I bring a pair of walking shoes and one fancier pair for dinners out. I wash my socks and underwear at night. Because I don't overload, I can find things quickly when I arrive, and repacking isn't a chore. My goal is to get down to one bag—which probably won't ever happen, but . . .

- *Cosmetics.* Get the tiniest bottles you can find and fill them with your shampoo, conditioner, facial cleanser, body lotion, Woolite for washing, and any other products you regularly use; this cuts the amount of baggage you have way down. Get some small bottles for any pills and vitamins, too.

- *Bring Your Own Pillow.* If you have trouble with your neck or back like I do, bringing along your own pillow will do wonders and ensure that you get a good night's sleep. It's also a handy thing to have while traveling; I sleep much better on a plane or train if I lean against my own pillow and avoid those small, scratchy ones.

- *Always Bring a Jacket or Coat.* No matter where I am going or what the climate, I always prepare for a change of weather. I went to Alaska with all my winter duds and they had a heat wave; I've also been to Florida when it is freezing, so one outfit that is suitable for the opposite weather condition of what you expect can be a great help. If you're traveling by plane, bring a coat or a big warm scarf or wrap that can double as a blanket on board with you, as it can get so cold on those long flights.

• *Your Carry-On.* Whether you're traveling by plane, train, or bus, a smartly packed carry-on or tote bag can make all the difference in whether you arrive exhausted or refreshed— and can also be a lifesaver if your luggage gets lost. My carry-on is so big these days that I usually have more gear for my flight than I do for the destination, and I often look like a Bedouin—but it's worth it to me to have what I need to be comfortable. I bring warm, comfy slippers; a black eyeshade; ear plugs; a small bottle of my favorite moisturizer; a shawl or sweater; books; iPod; glasses; makeup; a supply of healthy foods including sandwiches, fruit, granola bars, and other snacks I know I like; and then essentials, such as my wallet, ticket, cell phone, medications, glasses, contact lenses, and my passport if traveling abroad. When flying, I also bring along my plane medal of Saint Christopher (patron saint of protection) and a picture of Renny to have with me for take-off. Pre-arrival, my makeup comes out, the sweater and slippers come off, and after a quick ten minutes of sprucing up, a sleek, elegant woman emerges from the sprawl with book read, nap taken, food eaten, skin moisturized, and makeup applied—all in all quite happy.

Epilogue

When I was doing my play in Atlanta, I sent out a message to the *Guiding Light* fans on Twitter: "Am in Atlanta for two-week run of *Changing Shoes*. Love it here, though for some reason I've become obsessed with doughnuts."

Since my arrival, I had discovered Krispy Kreme—the famous doughnut chain that originated in the South and is known for their sinfully delicious glazed doughnuts, which they serve warm, right out of the oven. As luck would have it (or not have it), there was a Krispy Kreme two blocks from my hotel. Given my sweet tooth, I finally broke down and started stopping by daily for a pre- (or post-) rehearsal treat. But then one of the fans, a woman, tweeted me back: "Tina, I am a size twenty-two—take my word for it, do NOT go near the Krispy Kremes!"

This well-timed reminder of my bunny slipper days was all I needed to steer clear from then on—a romance between me and Krispy Kreme was not a good idea. But I loved this woman for what she'd done. She was looking out for me and warning me, one woman to another, about the perils of becoming entranced by warm glazed doughnuts (or chocolate glazed, or caramel glazed, or jelly-filled glazed . . . mmmm).

This book is YOUR warning. It is my message to you, the reader, to NOT let aging defeat you or slow you down. When I turned fifty, there was no one to warn me: "Tina, by not exercising, you're going to get fat." "Tina, by not sticking up for yourself at work, you're going to lose your role." "Tina, by settling for scruffy black flats, you're going to lose your confidence and your sense of self." Nobody told me that these things would happen. And as a result, I lost five years—five years that I could have spent doing just about anything, from auditioning for movies to hiking in Nepal, but instead spent sitting on the couch, mourning the loss of my youth and beauty, and feeling sorry for myself.

At any given moment in time, we have the power to transform ourselves and be whoever we want to be. We can put on the breaks and say, "No, it doesn't have to be like this," and change our shoes and choose another path. Looking back, I can honestly say that everything I've achieved in life—my career, my marriage, my son, my friends, and my most cherished accomplishments such as running marathons and reaching the summit on Kilimanjaro—has stemmed from a willingness to stay in the game. When given the opportunity to sit on the bench, even when the bench was oh-so-tempting, I summoned up my courage, found a new pair of shoes, and ran back out onto the playing field and took another chance.

There is a wonderful quote by George Sheehan, who is one of my favorite authors and who wrote many books about running: "The real sin is not dying, but living an unused life." And now I know that he is right. The years only go by faster as we age, and our days should be devoted to really LIVING. We need to continue taking leaps and expanding our boundaries and, when the mood strikes, wearing high heels and feeling fabulous. No matter what our age, we need to keep looking for ways to soar.

The reality is that we can't depend on much besides ourselves as we get older. We can't depend on our careers because they might go away. We can't depend on our children, because they grow up to follow their own paths. We can't depend on our looks because they're inevitably going to change. All we have is our own inner resilience to keep us going. We have to depend on our own two feet and hope that they will take us in the right direction. They can. And they WILL. But it's up to us. All we need is the perfect pair of shoes.

Acknowledgments

I feel so blessed to have the "girlfriends" I have; they have given so much to me and to this book through the life and laughter and wisdom and secrets they have brought into my life. To omit their names would make the book incomplete. Over the past year, I have stretched my friendships by staying inside to write rather than being outside and "playing"—I hope this huge THANK YOU rectifies that.

Many, many thanks to:

Abby, Adele, Alex, Alexandra, Alina, Alita, Alix, Allie, Amy, Andrea, Ann, Anne, Annie, Ashley, Audrey, Banany, Barrett, Becca, Bess, Beth, Betsy, Betty, Bobo, Bonnie, Brenda, Catherine, Cathy, Charlotte, Chris, Christy, Cindy, Consuleo, Corny, Courtney, Cristabel, Cynthia, Dana, Danielle, Debby, Diana, Diddle, Dinah, Donnell, Duane, Edith, Eliza, Ellen, Ellie, Elsie, Fran, Genie, Grace, Heather, Heidi, Helena, Israela, Jane, Jean, Jean again, Jeanne, Jennifer, Jill, Jodie, Joni, Josie, Kallie, Karen, Kate, Kathleen, Kathy, Kay, Kristin, Laura, Lia, Linda, Liz, Lucy, Lulie, Lydia, Maisie, Mandy, Marcie, Marge, Maria, Marty, Mary, Mary Jo, Maureen, Melinda, Missie, Monica, Nan, Nell, Nicole, Patsy, Patty, Penni, Polly, Priscilla, Reva, Rosie, Ruthie, Sally, Sandra, Sara, Sarah, Sheldon, Sherry, Siri, Slansky, Stephanie, Susan, Suzie, Talbot, Topsy, and Wendy.

All the world of *Guiding Light*—the cast, crew, production, and fans. I miss you so and always will.

The Web site geniuses of www.changingshoes.com: Jessica Lim and Laura Lim.

The wonderful people of Penguin and Gotham Books: Bill Shinker, Cara Bedick, Jessica Chun, Lisa Johnson, and my very own Beth Parker. Your sage advice guided me through every aspect of this book; I thank you and gratefully acknowledge all you have done for me.